A *MORE FOR YOUR* **MONEY** GUIDE

Free Food...
& More

Linda Bowman

PROBUS PUBLISHING COMPANY
Chicago, Illinois

© 1991, Probus Publishing Company

ALL RIGHTS RESERVED. No part of this publication may be reproduced, stored in a retrieval system, or transmitted by any means, electronic, mechanical, photocopying, recording or otherwise, without the prior written permission of the publisher and the copyright holder.

This publication is designed to provide accurate and authoritative information in regard to the subject matter covered. It is sold with the understanding that the publisher is not engaged in rendering legal, accounting or other professional service. If legal or other expert assistance is required, the services of a competent professional should be sought.

Library of Congress Cataloging in Publication Data Available.

ISBN   1-55738-220-4

Printed in the United States of America

BB

1   2   3   4   5   6   7   8   9   0

TABLE OF CONTENTS

CHAPTER 1
INTRODUCTION: FREEBIES AND BIG DISCOUNTS
ARE THERE FOR THE TAKING   1

CHAPTER 2
HOW TO GET FREEBIES AND DISCOUNTS ON FOOD AND
HOUSEHOLD GOODS   5

Clipping Coupons Really Pays Off!   5

Make a Killing with Refunds and Rebates   27

Alternatives to Saving at the Supermarket   45

Do It Yourself and Save   57

Make Your Own Convenience Foods   58

Alternatives to Store-Bought Baby Food   60

Save on Dining Out and Eat Like a King   62

CHAPTER 3
FREEBIES AND DISCOUNTS ON HEALTH AND BEAUTY PRODUCTS AND SERVICES 71

Vanity Can Be Cheap 71

Stay Healthy for Less 78

CHAPTER 4
FREEBIES AND SAVINGS IN THE HOME 99

Save on Your Energy Bills 99

Savings on Heating and Cooling Systems in the Home 101

Free Firewood for Your Fireplace and Wood-burning Stove 105

Free Christmas Trees, Wooden Poles, Posts and Seedlings 106

Free Information on Home Insulation 107

Windows and Window Treatments Can Save You Money, Too 109

Don't Be a Drip—Save Water and Save $$$ 110

Savings in the Garden 112

Be Safe and Save 113

Free Gas-Saving Tips for Your Car 115

Live in a Mansion—Rent-Free and for No Money Down 116

CHAPTER 5
READ, LISTEN AND LEARN A LOT FOR LESS   119

Free Magazines and Newsletters   119

Great Deals on Books   128

Savings on Movies, Cassette Tapes, and CD's   162

CHAPTER 1

INTRODUCTION: FREEBIES AND BIG DISCOUNTS ARE THERE FOR THE TAKING

If your family is like mine, it seems like we are imprisoned by a rising high cost of living that must be accepted as a fact of life that can't be changed. However, even though normal living expenses (i.e., food, home entertainment, utility bills, household goods) keep rising, individuals can reap *freebies* and incredible savings by learning simple methods and by gathering information that will enable them to keep, rather than spend, thousands of extra dollars each year.

There are discounts, bargains, and freebies in today's marketplace, offering consumers the chance to enjoy high quality, top-of-the-line products and services at a fraction of their normal cost or free, with no obligation or hidden costs. In fact, most of these amazing offers go wasted and unused, except by a few enlightened consumers, resulting in millions of dollars in unnecessary spending.

All you need to know are the places to go and the methods of smart shopping, so you and your family can begin taking advantage of the benefits that are available to "those in the know." These overlooked and little known, easy-to-use tools are your keys to freebies and fantastic savings on food, dining out, books and magazines, health and beauty products, and the ever-rising costs of running a household in the 1990s. Could your family make use of hundreds, even thousands of dollars in extra spending money each year? Could you benefit from receiving hundreds of free products and valuable information resulting in drastically cutting costs from your family budget? We believe we know *that* answer.

In fact, not only are we going to be giving you tools for super savings for your family, we are going to extend those savings to the other "members" of your family whose feeding alone supports an $8 billion a year industry. We're talking about your favorite four-legged friend—the family pet(s). Add to that figure the millions of dollars spent on health care, vitamins, toys and accessories for your pet and you have several excellent reasons for wanting to save money.

Wouldn't you rather cut your canine and feline bills in half or more and keep the savings for yourself? We think we know the answer to that one, too.

To begin with, we will show you how to stop being a victim of high food prices. Add to that the ridiculous cost of cosmetics, over-the-counter medicines and drugs, liquor, and other household goods (paper, plastics, soaps, and cleansers), and a monthly paycheck can nearly disappear purchasing these "bare necessities." Who can be happy about the way prices have been shooting through the roof? Most of us can identify with the "I can't believe I'm paying this much for one bag of stuff" look, when the supermarket cashier rings up our total for the "few things we've run out to the market for." As we hand her the money, we're usually thinking, "Did I buy all that?" Unfortunately, you didn't buy all that much, and what you did buy, you paid too much for.

Should you want to go out and enjoy yourself once or twice a week at a neighborhood restaurant or celebrate a special occasion—the extra dollars you may have saved from your food budget is quickly gone. However, we'll also show you how to eat out, guilt-free (without stealing from the family cookie jar) and save. We'll even show you how to enjoy terrific dining experiences for free!

Rising oil prices? Heating, electricity, and water bills going up? Gasoline prices on a roller coaster again? Little needs to be said about how we, the consumers, are at the mercy of the oil and

Chapter 1

energy producers and gasoline manufacturers. However, once again, there's no reason we should simply stand by as innocent victims. There are numerous, easy methods for saving on the high cost of using energy.

Our goal is to show you how to get as many goods and services either for free, or with as much savings as possible. Why spend your hard-earned dollers needlessly on everyday costs of living? Freebies and savings are there for the asking—every time you spend a dollar at the market, the drug store, the pet store, the liquor store. . . every time you buy a book, a magazine, a CD, or cassette. . . every time you pay an electric, gas, or water bill. . . every time you fill up at the gas pump. You could be saving nearly a dollar for every dollar you spend on these items and services adding up to a lot of free stuff.

In the following chapters we will take you through the steps in your journey towards unlimited savings. There aren't going to be a lot of complex or difficult rules along the way. In fact, this road is a lot simpler than Dorothy's well-known Road to Oz. And the rewards and benefits to you are 100 percent real—cash in your pocket.

Start small and build up. We'll show you how. It's fun, it feels good, and look at what you will have to show for your efforts: extra $$$ at the end of each month that will continue to grow the more you use our methods. (Don't worry that the savings may seem insignificant on each item. You will find that they can really add up over the year. One woman we discovered said that she saved enough to buy a new car with several years of savings!)

LET THE SAVINGS BEGIN!!

CHAPTER 2

HOW TO GET FREEBIES AND DISCOUNTS ON FOOD AND HOUSEHOLD GOODS

CLIPPING COUPONS REALLY PAYS OFF!

What would you think if you heard that someone was throwing money away with their garbage? Your first thought would probably be that this person must have a few loose marbles. Your second thought might be to find out where the person lived, so you could raid their garbage cans yourself.

Now, how would you feel if I told you that you are probably doing the very same thing—throwing your hard-earned cash right into the trash can? If you are like most people, it's true. You throw hundreds, maybe even thousands of dollars away each year. What's worse, you may not even know it.

Manufacturers distribute over 130 billion coupons to consumers annually, but less than 5 percent of them are redeemed. Americans throw away almost 38 billion dollars in unused coupons each and every year. For the typical family, this works out to over $2,200 lost every 12 months (smart shopper's, however, save more than $3 billion each year, with an average coupon value of 46 cents).

Just think what $2,200 could buy you: a camcorder, a new wardrobe, a stereo system, a vacation, even a big screen television.

Even a minimal investment of time in couponing will likely net you 20 percent savings off your weekly grocery bill. If you normally spend $100 per week at the supermarket, that works out to $1,040 in a year. If your food budget is closer to $200 per week, that's at least $2,080 in a year.

While these numbers are certainly nothing to sneeze at, my methods may double your savings. On a typical shopping trip, using the techniques outlined in this book, I routinely save up to 40 percent off my purchases, and sometimes even more. The result: an average of two hours a week spent clipping, sorting, and planning has earned me thousands of dollars each year.

A recent Sunday edition of the *Los Angeles Times* yielded $63.85 worth of cents-off coupons, $4.50 worth of coupons for free groceries, and $24.49 worth of refunds. Assuming they are redeemed at a store that doubles the face value of cents-off coupons, this is a potential savings of $156.69 for the cost of the newspaper. Of course, the coupons may not all be for items that you use. But even if you use only one out of every four, you will find an extra $39.17 in your wallet. You may even be able to trade the other three coupons for coupons you can use.

The coupons from your Sunday newspaper, in fact, represent only 25 percent of all coupons distributed. Another 50 percent come from daily newspapers, especially the weekly food sections. The rest may come from your favorite magazines, are printed on packages already in your cupboards, or show up unannounced in your mailbox.

In fact, the more coupons you use, the more you get. Many coupons are now coded so that manufacturers can tell which households redeem which coupons. They then use this information to send out packets of coupons, samples, and special offers to those who are the most likely to use them. Use coupons to buy dog food, for example, and you'll start to receive even more of them in your mailbox.

There are those who claim that coupons are self-defeating. Eliminate coupons, they say, and everyone's food bill will go down, because manufacturers will save money, and will pass their savings on to you.

In reality, coupons came into being because manufacturers wanted to make sure that any savings they offered made it into the hands of consumers. If a manufacturer simply cuts its wholesale price to the supermarkets, it has no way of ensuring that the market will pass on its savings to you. More likely, it could pocket some or all of the extra profit, and you would never see a dime of it. By issuing coupons, and keeping its wholesale prices consistent, a manufacturer knows the savings it offers go directly to you, the consumer.

"If we just reduce prices," explains Linda Jacobson, former product and merchandising manager for Amurol Products in Illinois, "there is no guarantee the reduction will be passed on from the retailer to the consumer. We would never know if our reductions were just added to the profits of retailers who never lowered their prices."

Martin Sloane, past president of the American Coupon Club, goes even further. "If manufacturers couldn't use one of their most successful promotion vehicles," he says, "they wouldn't lower prices. They'd buy more billboard space. I'd rather get that 25-cents-off coupon than pay for alternative forms of advertising. You can't eat a billboard."

According to Marion Joyce, a consumer advice columnist, "Coupons actually cost the manufacturer *less* than many other types of promotion and advertising techniques to get consumers' interest and stimulate sales of new and existing products."

Another strong supporter of couponing is Virginia Knauer, consumer adviser to Ronald Reagan during his presidency. She agrees with Martin Sloane that manufacturers would not lower their prices if coupons were not offered. As far as using coupons, she says, "I love it. I think it has a great benefit for consumers in these inflationary times... I think [consumers] can see the benefit of getting 40 or 50 cents off on a can of coffee they'd buy anyway. That's just good old American competition."

In reality, only about three cents out of every ten dollars you spend at the market goes to cover the cost of coupons. That's only three tenths of 1 percent of your food bill. If your couponing saves you even 20 percent a week, you still come out far ahead. Worse still, nonusers lose not only the value of the coupons and double-coupons they throw away, but they save the manufacturers from having to pay handling fees to the markets. At $.08 per coupon, that's like giving manufacturers a $9 billion Christmas gift each year. It's not that I'm stingy, but I would rather choose whom I give those kinds of presents to!

Other naysayers imply that any savings coupon-users earn are offset by the amount of time they spend clipping and organizing. "Time is money," they say. Time *is* money. Which is why I prefer to spend two hours a week clipping and organizing coupons while watching television or talking on the phone—time that would otherwise be wasted. When those two hours result in a $40 or $50 savings, I figure that I'm getting paid to watch T.V.!

In the end, even the pessimists admit that as long as coupons exist, it's downright silly not to use them.

Types of Coupons

There are four main categories that coupons fall into: cents-off, free items, free items with purchase, and store coupons. Savvy coupon-users will use all of these to maximize their savings.

"Cents-off" coupons are the most common, and are probably what you picture when you think of coupons. These offer the consumer a certain amount of money off the purchase of a particular product. Purely at face value, they may be worth anywhere from $.10 to $2—or more. Remember, however, that their true value is *doubled* when you take advantage of stores' double-coupon offers.

You will also find coupons for free items. These are often for trial sizes of new items, or new varieties of familiar items, but more and more frequently, manufacturers are distributing coupons for full-size items. ReaLemon recently printed coupons good for free lemon juice in local Sunday newspaper inserts. No other purchase was required. All you had to do was take the coupon to the store and walk out with as many bottles as you had coupons. It goes without saying that these are the most highly prized of all types of coupons. How can you top getting something absolutely for free?

Some coupons offer free groceries when you purchase a particular item. They may be specific, such as offering a free gallon of milk with your purchase of the company's breakfast cereal, or they may be applicable toward any groceries, up to a specified dollar amount, when you buy the company's product. These are used by manufacturers to get consumers who already buy one of their company's products to try other products. Breakfast cereals, in fact, are frequently featured, where the purchase of one variety earns a free box of another variety.

These "free with purchase" coupons are valuable when the product to be purchased is one you need, or would like to have. Be careful, though. If you are obligated to buy something you know you won't use, you may not be getting a bargain—no matter how much money the coupon saves you. You may be better off using a cents-off coupon for an item you really want than paying for an item that will sit on your pantry shelf, unused, simply because its purchase earned you something else for free.

Finally, there are store, or retailer, coupons. These are coupons that are not issued by a product's manufacturer, but, rather, by the store that sells it. They may require a minimum purchase, but they usually represent excellent values. This is also one of the few times you'll see coupons for basics. For instance, my local market periodically offers free eggs or a loaf of bread with a minimum purchase.

Though they can't be doubled, store coupons can often be used in conjunction with manufacturers' coupons, thus multiplying their savings potential substantially. You may, for example, find a store coupon for $.50 off a half-gallon of ice cream. If you also have a manufacturer's cents-off coupon for $.25, and shop where your cents-off coupons are doubled, using both coupons will save you a full dollar off the price of the ice cream.

Large supermarkets aren't the only ones that issue store coupons. Smaller, independent markets, which are generally more expensive than the large chains, use store coupons as an incentive to keep their loyal customers. A nearby independent market advertises "$.89 for a dozen eggs" coupons almost weekly. At $2.39 per dozen (or more) at the supermarket, the savings are clear. Remember, too, that if you are lucky enough to have a supermarket near you that accepts other stores' coupons, you can take advantage of these valuable offers without making a special trip to the store that advertises them.

For what kinds of products do you find coupons? Nearly everything. It used to be that coupons for meat, poultry, and produce were rare. But since brand-name meat and poultry have become increasingly popular, coupons for these products have become more commonplace. A recent promotion even included a coupon for $.25 off the price of an avocado!

Still, more coupons are distributed for some items than for others. You will find the most popular coupon offers for: coffee, tea, and cocoa; household supplies (including paper products and cleaning supplies); soups, baby food, and prepared food; pet food; and breakfast cereals. So many coupons are distributed for these products, in fact, that I never pay full price for them—and neither should you.

Double Coupons and Other Great Deals

It's worth your while to find a store that will double all of your cents-off coupons. In the past, stores merely printed a few coupons in their weekly ads that, when redeemed with cents-off coupons, doubled their value. Recently, though, some stores have taken to doubling all manufacturers cents-off coupons, without requiring any printed double coupons. You may even be

Chapter 2

lucky enough to find a store that triples manufacturers' coupons, though they are becoming increasingly rare.

If the store closest to you doesn't offer unlimited double coupons, consider driving the extra distance to one that does at least once a month, and do most of your shopping for frequently-couponed items there.

Many markets limit the value of your coupon, doubled or not, to the price of the item. Or they may only double up to $1.00, even if the cents-off coupon is for more. This protects them from having to give you money back if the coupon value exceeds the item's price. If coffee is on sale for $1.25, for example, and you have a $.75 coupon at a store that offers double coupons, the store may only give you credit for $1.25. The coffee is still yours for free.

Some stores do not place these limits on couponers. If you are lucky enough to have one nearby, you may even be able to make money when you shop. That same can of coffee could actually earn you 25 cents. Needless to say, these stores are my favorites!

Stores that not only offer unlimited double coupons, but also accept other stores' coupons are where the biggest savings can be found. Hughes Markets, in Southern California, for instance, accept store coupons from any other local supermarket, *and* offer unlimited double coupons.

Getting Started

To begin with, you will need a box and a pair of scissors. As you clip coupons out, just toss them in the box. Don't worry about sorting the coupons at this point; we will deal with that later. For now, let's focus on finding as many of these money-savers as possible.

Take a good look at the items in your kitchen. There is an excellent chance that items already on your shelves have coupons printed right on their packages, or stuffed inside. On-pack and in-pack coupons are a great way to start out, because they are for items you already use.

A quick browse through my kitchen turned up several coupons for cereal, both hot and cold, and other coupons for pasta, bread, cheese, and pet food. These coupons are often designed so that it is impossible to remove them from the package without spilling corn flakes or macaroni all over the kitchen floor. You can avoid this by simply examining all empty boxes, bottles, and bags before you throw them away.

Next, since half of all coupons are distributed in daily editions of local newspapers, find out which day your paper publishes its food section. Generally these sections come out every Wednesday or Thursday.

Look through the food section thoroughly. This is the best place to find store or retailer coupons; they are usually buried in the stores' advertisements. This is one of the least expensive ways for manufacturers to advertise their products, too, and they take full advantage. Almost every week I find coupons for two or more brands of soft drinks, which alone pay for the cost of the newspaper many times over.

Another 25 percent of all coupons can be found in the free-standing colorful inserts in Sunday papers. Most of the coupons in Sundays' inserts are cents-off coupons, but this is still my best source for free-item and free-item-with-purchase coupons. Don't be surprised if the coupons in your Sunday paper exceed $75 at face value, before doubling.

Nearly sixteen billion additional coupons are printed in magazines every year. Focus your attention next on any family, fashion, or health magazines that you have sitting around and you will turn up quite a few valuable coupons. Ask your neighbors if they would mind passing on their already-read magazines. A recent issue of *Woman's Day* held $1.75 in coupon savings, worth $3.50 when doubled—and the magazine cost me nothing, as a neighbor was throwing it away.

Also check your mailbox. We may complain about the amount of "junk" mail we get, but smart couponers know that the mailbox can be a gold mine. Major manufacturers often send out free

Chapter 2

samples of new products they are putting on the market, or valuable coupons for both new and familiar items. Many manufacturers even hire companies that specialize in distributing coupons and free samples through the mail. CAROL WRIGHT, 1000 Donnelley Drive, Elm City, NC 27822-1000, is among the best-known. They send out packets of coupons and samples year-round to the people on their mailing list. A recent Carol Wright mailing contained $2.25 worth of cents-off coupons (worth $4.50 doubled), in addition to other special offers.

If you are not already on their mailing list, write and ask them to send you a "SHOPPER'S SURVEY" to fill out. In this manner, they are able to tailor future mailings to your exact needs.

SELECT & SAVE, P.O. Box 9008, Hicksville, NY 11801, is another major distributor of direct-mail coupons. A recent packet contained $5.95 worth of cents-off coupons, a free trial size coupon worth $.99, and a free-with-purchase coupon worth $.45. They, too, ask that you fill out a survey so they can send you coupons for products that suit your needs.

Finally, look for coupons in the supermarket itself. Often manufacturers set up tasting stands showcasing one or more of their products, and offer free in-store samples and coupons. If coupons are handed out, add them to your coupon box. Don't be tempted to buy the item on the spot; stores may jack up their prices on these items, if they think consumers will be redeeming the coupons that day.

A recent innovation in couponing is the introduction of checkstand coupons. Upon ringing up your order, a computerized unit automatically prints out coupons for items similar to those purchased. A purchase of cat food may trigger the printing of a flea-collar coupon, a purchase of disposable diapers may produce a baby food coupon. These coupons may be financed by the retailer or by the manufacturer, so check them carefully to see whether they can be redeemed only at face value or can be doubled.

A firm called THE SAVING SPOT (TSS) has introduced an electronic unit that distributes manufacturers' coupons in the stores. Shoppers punch in their personal access code, provided by the store, and are issued up to 32 different coupons right then and there. The computer keeps track of what you buy, and this information may then be used to mail out even more coupons. TSS is currently being used by markets in the Southeastern United States, including Kroger, Cub Foods, and Big Star.

Supermarkets may also team up with local charity organizations to produce and distribute coupon books. Several West Coast stores, including the Lucky chain and Ralph's Grocery Stores, have gotten together with the City of Hope Medical Research Center and produced what they call "Coupons of Hope." The "Coupons of Hope" booklets contain around $65 worth of manufacturers' coupons, which can be doubled. An added benefit of using these coupons is that the manufacturers featured agree to make a small donation to the charity for each coupon redeemed. Charity tie-ins are also frequently featured in Sunday coupon inserts.

As a kind of informal way to exchange unwanted coupons, shoppers in some areas leave coupons that they are not going to use on the shelf next to the featured item. If they have coupons for two different brands of dishwasher detergent, for instance, they may buy the one they prefer and leave the other coupon behind. Some stores even have coupon exchange bins or boxes expressly for this purpose.

One more thing: brand loyalty and couponing don't mix. The only way to earn big bucks at the supermarket is to be willing to try brands other than those you normally use. More often than not, there is little difference in quality from one name brand to another. An added benefit to this necessary flexibility is that you and your family get to try all sorts of new brands, foods, and flavors, and save money at the same time.

Chapter 2

Now What?

By now you should have a good-sized stack of coupons in your box. You are probably surprised at the potential savings they represent. But trying to use them without some system of organization will end up driving you crazy. At this point you must do some serious sorting in order to find coupons for any one item on your grocery list.

You will need either an accordion file or another box, with dividers. A shoebox will do, and dividers can be made out of any leftover piece of cardboard. Try cutting up empty cereal or other boxes (after you check them for coupons, of course!).

Begin sorting your coupons into stacks by category: pet supplies, desserts, cereals, cleaning supplies, paper and plastic products, dairy items, canned goods—whatever categories suit your shopping needs. Categories should be fairly specific. Don't try to oversimplify things. Your goal is to make it as easy as possible to find the coupons you want when you want them.

As you are sorting, pull out any coupons that have very short expiration dates, i.e., within two or three weeks. These coupons go in a separate section in the very front of your box. This will help you avoid missing good deals because a coupon has expired without your noticing.

The process of sorting out all those slips of paper can be daunting. But, once your coupon box is set up, the time needed to spend maintaining it is minimal. Unpleasant as it is to sort out hundreds of coupons, it is a one-time task, and a necessary step to becoming a successful couponer. From now on, you will be sorting your coupons once or twice a week, and it will take much less time.

Once you have your coupons sorted and stacked, label your dividers and file the coupons. Try putting the categories in the same order as your supermarket's aisles. That way, when you pull out coupons for a shopping trip, they are ready to go.

Now that the hard part is over, you will only need to spend a couple of hours a week on your coupons to reap incredible savings on your grocery bills.

Putting Your Shopping List Together

By now you know that one of the keys to getting hundreds or thousands of dollars worth of free food is organization. You have already organized your coupons. Now you need to organize your shopping list.

During the week, keep a list of items that you are running out of. Hang a pad of paper and a pen on your refrigerator, with a reminder to mark down anything that gets used up. This will save you from having to make mad dashes to convenience stores—and pay exorbitant prices—when you realize you have forgotten to buy something at the market.

Before you go to the market, go through your kitchen, and note anything on which you are running low. Don't forget things like cleaning supplies, toilet paper, and shampoo. These items are expensive if you pay full price, and there are coupons offered for them nearly every week.

Now sit down with your list, your coupon file, and the supermarket's weekly advertisement. Your goal is to match up as many items from your list as possible with coupons from your file. Ideally, you will be able to tie in a store special on the item, too. For example, a local market recently had a special on a half-gallon of juice. Normally selling for $2.99, it was on sale for $2.49. I had a coupon for $.75 off. The store doubled my coupon, and I paid only $1.00 for the juice and saved 67 percent!

In the coupon world, matching store specials with coupons is often referred to as a "double-play." Do this at a store that also doubles your manufacturers' cents-off coupons, as in the example above, and it's called a "super double-play." A "triple-play" is when you buy an item on special with a coupon, and use the proof-of-purchase to send for a refund from the manufacturer.

Chapter 2
17

Using these techniques will earn you freebies and substantial savings immediately.

Pull out all of the coupons for each item on your list. If one of the brands is on special, make a note of it. But bring the coupons for other brands with you. Often stores have what they call "unadvertised specials"—and their prices may be even lower than those of the advertised specials. Keep an eye out for specials that are marked "one to a customer," or have other strict quantity limits; this is a tip-off that the item is an excellent buy.

Once you have gone through your list, pulled coupons for the items you need, and noted potential "double-plays," you are ready to head to the supermarket.

Raking in the Savings

You've clipped, sorted, and filed. You've scoured newspapers, magazines, stores, and your mailbox for money-saving coupons. You've spent time poring over the food section of your newspaper, matching up store specials with manufacturers' and retailers' coupons. Now comes the payoff.

Place your coupons in an envelope, and bring two extra envelopes with you. Mark one "used" and the other "not used."As you go through the store, you will place the coupons into one or the other of these envelopes. This will relieve you of having to sort them out at the checkstand, facing both impatient stares from the customers in line behind you and the possibility of forgetting to redeem coupons for items you have bought.

If you have a calculator bring it along for figuring out per-unit prices, which tell you the package size or brand that will save you the most money. As you get more involved in couponing, you may find it worthwhile to invest in a small coupon holder.

Following these simple rules while you are in the supermarket will get you the most savings:

First, stick to your list and avoid impulse buys, unless they are exceptional values. Markets are planned so that you have to walk past the most tempting items to get to the necessities. Don't fall for it. This can wreak havoc with your food budget.

Second, look for packages that offer additional coupons. Different packages of the same item may have varying offers on them. Some boxes of the same breakfast cereal, for instance, may advertise merchandise you can send for, while others may display cents-off coupons for future purchases. In most cases, I choose the box with the coupons.

Third, always figure out the per-unit prices of different sizes and brands before you buy. Over the years, we have been led to believe that larger sizes represent better deals by such labels as "economy size." But larger sizes are not necessarily more economical. They are often priced even higher per unit than are smaller packages. This is especially true when you are shopping with coupons.

To get to the per-unit price, take the price of the item and subtract the value of your coupons and double-coupons. Now divide this number by the units the package contains. (For many products, this will be ounces. For items like paper towels, it is square feet. For other items, like paper cups and plates, you will want to use the number of cups or plates the package holds.) You will end up with a per-unit price. Compare these numbers to find out which is really the least expensive.

For example, six ounces of a particular brand of instant coffee may cost $3.29, or $.55 an ounce. A ten-ounce jar is priced at $4.99, or $.50 an ounce. Normally, the larger size would be the better buy. But coupons change things. Let's say I have a coupon worth $.75 off the coffee, and the store will double my savings. This brings the six-ounce jar down to $1.79, or 30 cents an ounce, and the ten-ounce jar down to $3.49, or $.35 an ounce. Clearly, once coupon savings are figured in, buying the smaller jar makes more sense.

Fourth, when you find a great buy on a nonperishable item, like household products or canned food, stock up. Although you are limited to one manufacturer's coupon per item, you can usually buy as many items as you have coupons for. If soup is on sale for $.49 a can, and you have five coupons, each worth $.30, buy five cans. Depending on your store's double coupon policy, the soup will either be free or it will earn you $.11 a can. That's smart couponing.

What can you save? I recently went to an unlimited double coupon store for my weekly shopping, and purchased a variety of items. I bought toilet paper and tissues, produce and meat, soft drinks, pet food, and frozen foods, among many other things. When the checker rang up my order, it totaled $91.61. Without blinking, I handed her my stack of coupons. Shoppers behind me looked on in curiosity. By the time my cents-off, double, store, and free product coupons were figured in, my total was down to $52.58, including tax. I had saved 43 percent—even without counting the store's specials. Even the checker was impressed.

For the BIG Bucks: Coupon Exchanging

As you begin to see sizable discounts at the grocery store, the potential for even higher savings becomes clear. Up until now, you have been limited to the coupons available in your area, and in the newspapers, magazines, and "junk" mail you have been able to easily get your hands on.

Often manufacturers vary their promotions by area. One city, for instance, may receive coupons for free products, while others receive small cents-off coupons for the same product, or are ignored altogether. This practice is frustrating, but it can be beat.

Many couponing enthusiasts have turned to formal or informal coupon exchange clubs as a way to obtain coupons for the items they use. If you are taking advantage of the coupons left behind in your supermarket, you are doing this already. You simply trade coupons for items you don't buy for coupons for items you do. One family may have a pet, but no need for disposable diapers, while another may have a baby, but no need for pet food. Get the two together, and both come out ahead.

The easiest way to do this is informally, among your friends, neighbors, and relatives. Try passing along coupons that you can't use to friends and family members, and at the same time letting them know you would like to have any coupons that they are not going to use.

One couponer recommends that you "simply pass the word among your friends and neighbors to come for coffee and bring whatever coupons . . . they would be willing to trade." Try to get as many participants as possible—nine or ten, if you can. When the group realizes the how much money they can save, they may be willing to meet once a month to trade unwanted coupons.

This group approach has become so popular, in fact, that national coupon exchange organizations have sprung up all over. JOY COUPON EXCHANGE, P.O. Box 8216, Inglewood, CA

90308, is one. For a $15 annual fee, members have access to coupons from all over the country.

Karen Crump, the exchange's president, explains: "Every week, members nationwide cut coupons out of their Sunday paper, or other coupon circular, keeping the coupons they want and putting aside the unwanted ones. Before the fifteenth day of each month, members mail us their unwanted coupons . . . In return, we mail them coupons they need and use . . . that have been received from other members nationwide." A questionnaire tells the exchange which coupons you want to receive.

Coupon exchange clubs are often advertised in classified advertisements in the backs of magazines and in local newspapers. Before you join, compare membership fees, how many people belong to the club, and any other restrictions that may affect how the club will work for you. Single people may find that the membership fees negate the benefits of belonging to a club, but those who shop for larger families may find them a tremendous help in cutting their food bills.

It is estimated that the average family spends about one quarter of its total budget in the supermarket. Cutting 20, 30 or 40 percent—or more—adds up quickly. Even if you save only $20 a week, you will have over $1,000 to show for your efforts by year end—and with the techniques in this book, you can save much more.

Still need convincing? Set up a bank account for your coupon savings. After each shopping trip, deposit the money you saved by couponing into this account. Within weeks, you will be able to see just how quickly your clipping, sorting, organizing, and comparison shopping is paying off. You will be saving money for a vacation, a new stereo system, or simply to ease a too-tight budget, and enjoying free food all the while!

A SAMPLING OF RECENT COUPON OFFERS

Offer	Percent Savings*
Household Products	
Free Sparkle paper towels with purchase of 2 Lysol cleaning products	100 %
Free Glad Cling Wrap with purchase of 2 Glad-Lock zipper storage bags	100
Free STP gas treatment with purchase of 2 gallons of Prestone anti-freeze/coolant	100
$1.00 off Fresh Start laundry detergent	48
$.35 off Tide laundry detergent	25
$.40 off Clorox 2 bleach	36
$.35 off Hefty Cinch Sak trash bags	22
$.50 off Lysol deodorizing spray	46
$.50 off 2 packs of Energizer batteries	25
Personal Products	
$.50 off Aqua-Fresh toothpaste	67
$.40 off Scope mouthwash	29
$1.00 off Dristan	50
$1.00 off Sinutab	46
$1.00 off Chlor-Trimeton	61
$1.00 off Tylenol Cold Effervescent	40

*"Percent savings" represents savings off regular prices, assuming cents-off coupons are redeemed at a store offering unlimited double coupons.

continued...

Offer	Percent Savings*
$.50 off Advil ibuprofen	44
$.50 off Bayer aspirin	44
$1.00 off Jheri Redding hair products	65
$1.00 L'Oréal Colorvive Technicare shampoo or conditioner	57
$.40 off Silkience shampoo or conditioner	26
$.40 off Mink Difference hair spray	28
Free Carefree Longs with purchase of 2 packages of Carefree Panty Shields	100
Free panty liners with purchase of 2 Stayfree or Sure & Natural products	100
$1.00 off Speed Stick antiperspirant	87
$.50 off Lady Speed Stick antiperspirant (plus $1.00 refund offer)	100
$.40 off Bic Metal razors	62
Free No Nonsense pantyhose with purchase of 2 Neutrogena body care products	100

Dairy Products

Free Carnation Evaporated Milk with purchase of Saran Wrap	100
Free half-gallon of milk with purchase of Quaker 100% Natural cereal	100
Free gallon of milk with purchase of 2 boxes of Cap'n Crunch cereal	100
Free half-gallon of milk with purchase of Almond Delight cereal	100

continued...

Offer	Percent Savings*
Free Parkay margarine quarters with purchase of Parkay spread, soft margarine, or whipped margarine	100
$.50 off Kraft Light Singles processed cheese slices	50
$.30 off Coffee-mate Liquid nondairy creamer	87
Beverages	
Free Maxwell House filter packs with purchase of Maxwell House ground	100
$.75 off Nescafé instant coffee	47
$.75 off Melitta ground coffee	54
$.35 off Lipton tea	26
$.40 off Carnation Hot Cocoa Mix	24
$.40 off Kool-Aid Kool Bursts	50
Free Hawaiian Punch with purchase of 2 bottles and 1 bag of Chex-Mix	100
Free Hawaiian Punch with purchase of 2 64-ounce bottles	100
$.75 off Chiquita juice blends	50
$.35 off Dole pineapple juice	52
$.30 off 2-liter bottle of Coke, Sprite, or Dr Pepper	50
Sweet Stuff	
Free Jell-O gelatin with purchase of 2	100
Free Néstle candy bar with purchase of 6	100

continued...

Offer	Percent Savings*
$.35 off Dreyer's Grand ice cream	27
$.30 off Dole Fruit 'n Juice bars	21
Bread	
Free bread with purchase of Van de Kamp's frozen fish and Progresso soup	100
Free bakery goods with purchase of Coffee-mate and Hill's Brothers coffee	100
Free Italian bread with purchase of Contadina pasta and sauce	100
$.35 off Sahara pita bread	71
$.30 off Roman Meal bread	47
Cereals	
Free Kellogg's Corn Flakes with purchase of Folger's ground coffee	100
Free Peanut Butter Crunch with purchase of Cap'n Crunch	100
Free Double Chex with purchase of Rice or Corn Chex	100
Free Great Grains with purchase of 1	100
$.40 off Cheerios	25
$.40 off Fruit & Fibre	25
$.40 off Almond Delight	26
$.40 off Total	27
$.40 off Lucky Charms	25
continued...	

Offer	Percent Savings*
$.40 off Crispix	26
$.40 off Cinnamon Toast Crunch	25
Pet Supplies	
Free groceries with purchase of Chuck Wagon Lean	100
Free groceries with purchase of Purina Kibbles & Chunks	100
Free groceries with purchase of Purina Gravy	100
Free can of Grand Gourmet with purchase of 3	100
Free can of Pedigree Food for Puppies with purchase of dry Pedigree Food for Puppies	100
Free can of Pedigree Choice Cuts with purchase of Pedigree Mealtime	100
Free package of Snausages with purchase of Kibbles & Bits	100
Free can of Whiskas Select Entrees with purchase of 2	100
$.40 off Kit 'N Kaboodle	62
$.30 off Cat Chow	47
$.35 off Tender Vittles	50
$.30 off 6 cans of Fresh Catch	23
$.30 off Jonny Cat cat litter	40

MAKE A KILLING WITH REFUNDS AND REBATES

How would you like to have major U.S. companies sending you checks each week? Apart from couponing, which nets you instant cash savings at the check-out counter, manufacturers' refund offers are where you stand to make a substantial sum of money. In fact, becoming a skilled, savvy refunder can sometimes earn you more money than a job where you had to pay out expenses for transportation, child care, housework, and a separate work wardrobe. To become a refunder, all you need is an organized system, a few hours a week, some inexpensive supplies, a local mail box and you're in business.

Refunds and rebates (they mean the same thing in manufacturers' lingo) differ from coupons in that you have to mail the refund form and other required items back to the company in order to receive your refund. You will receive your refund within 4 to 8 weeks in one of the following forms:

- Cash or check. These refunds offer the highest value, anywhere from $1 to $10 depending on how many products are eligible in the refund offer.

- Coupons good for "cents-off" discounts (usually worth $1 or more) or a percentage off subsequent purchases of your original product. Or your coupon may entitle you to receive your next purchase for free.

- Coupons good for free products other than those you originally purchased (e.g., milk, bread, produce, film, batteries, and pantyhose.) Calendars, especially, are a popular item in free refund offers.

- "Buy one, two or three, and get one free" coupons. These require proofs of purchase (also called POPs or UPC Codes) from several of the same item. You don't have to buy them all at once. You can save the POPs until you have enough to send in for a free product.

- In-store *"cents-off"* coupons good for additional savings plus your refund check or discount coupons.
- Promotional items, purchased at cost or below wholesale by the manufacturer, that you receive with proofs of purchase, a form, and a set amount of money. For example, a detergent manufacturer might offer a refund for a back-pack or set of towels for $5.95 (supposedly less than the retail price) plus three proofs of purchase from boxes of detergent. These offers should be carefully examined. If you don't need the promotional item, you could be paying more in the long run for the products to collect the required number of POPs.

Most of us have seen refund offers and forms in the coupon supplements that come with your Sunday newspaper. Your local supermarket or drugstore may have a special carousel or bulletin board where they display offers for products they carry. If you've ever looked closely at the forms and their list of requirements, you may have been intimidated by what seems to be a lot of impossible rules and regulations. Don't be taken in, it's a lot simpler than it appears.

In fact, one reason manufacturers put so many conditions in their offers making them look complicated and difficult, is to discourage *too* many consumers from taking advantage of their generous offers. On the one hand, if a larger number of consumers participated in redeeming offers, the manufacturers would have to pay out millions of dollars more than they are doing at present. On the other hand, they know that the percentage of people who are "regular" refunders is small, so in recent years the number of offers and their value have increased significantly. Their objective is to lure you with tasty cash offers, hoping you will buy their products, but not *follow through* on the refund offer. And most of the time, they accomplish their goal with the consumer losing by paying full price for an expensive supermarket or drugstore item.

In addition to luring you into buying their products, manufacturers are hoping you will switch from "Brand X" to their brand. However, refunders cannot afford to be brand loyal all the time, especially since there are so many products that perform nearly the same. As with couponing you need to be flexible if you are going to become a serious refunder.

Refund offers also help increase a product's sales, help manufacturers gain more shelf space, increase their visibility through promotions and advertising, and give them the opportunity to tie-in with other manufacturers for a wider range of offers. And when they join "cents-off" coupons with refund and sweepstakes offers, manufacturers increase our incentive to use their product by offering even more savings.

We will show you how to take advantage of these offers, consistently and regularly, reaping the benefits so generously offered us each week. Remember, refunding is most profitable if you can purchase the item(s) when they are on sale, thus saving at the check-out counter and receiving a refund in the mail. You can make a real killing, though, and even end up getting the product for free, if you buy it on sale, use the in-store coupon at a market that doubles coupon values, and then send away for your cash refund. We believe free groceries, household goods, medicines, liquor and cosmetics are worth a few dedicated hours a week! Just think of how you'll feel each time you open your mail box and see all those checks, waiting to be cashed, as a reward for your time and effort.

Where to Find Refund/Rebate Offers

We already mentioned that refund offers appear in the Sunday supplement coupon inserts. These bright, splashy advertisements announce new products or sweepstakes or come with coupons as incentives to try products that have lots of competition on the supermarket shelves.

As we mentioned before, a lot of people are inclined to throw away those "junk mail" packets of valuable coupons and refund offers. You may not use them all, but why throw away money for products you normally use or would like to try? Many packets contain discounts for neighborhood services, such as carpet cleaning, dog grooming, auto tuning, and dry cleaning. Take a few minutes to figure out which ones to add to your refunding/couponing bank and which ones to throw away.

Individual offers also come in the mail, often in the form of sample mailings with follow-up coupons and refund offers. Don't just use the sample and toss out the rest. If you like the product and want to try it again, why not save on your initial purchase?

"Women's magazines" and general consumer magazines are also a good source for refunding. Look through current copies of *Good Housekeeping, McCalls, Better Homes and Gardens, Ladies' Home Journal,* and any specialty magazines that focus on your interests or hobbies. If you subscribe to any of these magazines, you are probably receiving bonus coupons. Manufacturers often put extra coupons into copies that are mailed to subscribers.

Supermarket and drugstore bulletin boards and carousels (often placed in the back of a store or in an inconvenient corner, again discouraging takers) carry a variety of current offers. This is one of the easiest ways of finding out about the latest round of refunds. Check the bulletin board at your supermarket and start ripping off those refund request forms. You can collect lots of original forms (more about forms later) for free without having to send away for them or go through a refund club.

Ask your local store manager for a list of refunds. He should have a current list available. Make a copy for your own files or ask if he has extras.

Refund request forms also appear on shelves as tear-off pads next to or near the products for which they are making the offer.

Some manufacturers place hanging tags and booklets on bottle necks containing refund forms along with recipes and other product information. Don't limit your search for refund forms to your market and drug store. Toy stores, pet stores, hardware stores, appliance stores, lumber stores, and home-building and improvement stores also advertise manufacturers rebates.

You probably have some refund forms in your cupboards at home right now. Check the sides and backs of boxes. Look inside packages for coupons and offers buried inside the contents. Some offers are printed on the *inside* of cardboard boxes or labels on canned goods. Next time you go to the market, check for specially marked packages with refund forms. Not all boxes are printed with offers, so you may have to hunt for a box with savings.

You can learn about special rebate offers through television and radio advertisements, although most of these are limited to big ticket items, such as cars and appliances, due to the expense of radio and TV commercial time. Still, some manufacturers cooperate with local merchants or chain stores on advertising "limited time only" rebates on products that are carried in your area. Many of these same stores advertise "factory" or "manufacturers" rebates on merchandise that is about to be replaced with next year's models. Televisions, stereos, VCRs and small appliances are purchased at the regular or sale price, with the mail-in refund resulting in considerable additional savings to the buyer.

Again, it's very important to remember to "follow through" with sending in for your refund. You will be missing some outstanding opportunities for saving hundreds and possibly thousands of dollars a year. If you do not take full advantage of rebate offers, you can really lose out by paying full price for products when you might have been able to save more buying other brands on sale.

Finally, you can find out about refunds through refunding newsletters and magazines and by joining refunding clubs and conventions. You can find these publications and organizations listed in your telephone book Yellow Pages under "Barter and Trade Exchanges" or in your local shopper/pennysaver newspaper.

How to Organize Your Refunding Materials

This is the most important part of becoming a successful refunder. You need a system. Whether you use the one we outline or one your devise for yourself, you must have a system or method of organizing your materials.

We suggest you create a "refund bank" to collect items required by offers. Your deposits will be your refund forms, POPs, etc. You will be making withdrawals as you send away for refunds. And you will be closing out accounts as you discard or trade any offers that have expired or you decide you don't want. (Your real bank account, of course, will be growing all the while as you deposit the valuable checks you will be receiving.)

You can separate the refund request forms you collect by dollar amount, alphabetically by product type, by supermarket and nonsupermarket offers, or by expiration date within groups. Similar to organizing coupons, you can use a "recipe" box, a shoe box with dividers, or an accordion file (cover the printed labels with your own.) A three-ring binder and large envelopes punched with holes will also work. Label each envelope or use colored plastic tabs to identify the contents.

Many offers require you to send a SASE (self-addressed, stamped envelope) along with your proofs of purchase and forms. Save yourself a lot of hassle by having a roll of self-sticking labels made with your name and address. Make up a big batch of SASEs and stick them in one of your compartments.

You will also be required to send in varying parts of boxes, labels, and packages that include the UPC code as your proof of purchase (the Universal Product Code or bar code is the little printed number surrounding a series of heavy lines). Other items you may need to save include seals, neck bands, plastic wrappers, boxtops, labels, caps or cap liners, ingredient panels, weight statements, nutritional information panels or certain words that are printed on the package or box.

In reviewing thousands of refund offers we have found that nearly every one of them required the UPC symbol and your original, dated cash register receipt with the item(s) circled. Some require sending in parts from two or more related products, usually produced by the same company.

By the way, you may have noticed coupons appearing on the backs of your supermarket or drugstore register receipts. These are good for discounts or savings at local establishments. Before destroying those receipts for the coupons, check whether the purchase in your refund offer has been rung up on the other side. Remember, most forms require "original" receipts and won't accept photocopies.

Now you need to organize your register receipts and the parts of the product packaging that are required. Save as much of the printed parts on boxes and packages as possible. Cut those parts out, flatten them, and throw out the rest. For bottles, soak off all labels, keeping them and the cap or top. With smaller boxes, keep the whole box. Store them in paper bags or cardboard boxes from the market alphabetically by brand names and/or categories. Keep a written master list of what you have collected by product offer and expiration date (or whatever system works for you), to help you stay organized.

What You Need to Do to Receive Your Rebate

It is quite common for refund requests to be rejected because the consumer has not complied *exactly* with the requirements of the offer. This is very important. If you don't do everything just the way they want you to, you run the risk of wasting a lot of time and money. After reading the fine print on a few dozen offers, you will become familiar with "refund lingo" and the terms and conditions that accompany nearly every offer. Some common ones include:

- Limit one or two requests per person, family, household, organization (where allowed), or address.
- Facsimiles, photocopies, or other mechanical reproductions of proofs of purchase, refund certificates and cash register receipts will not be accepted.
- Offer cannot be combined with any other offer.
- Allow four to ten weeks for delivery.
- Offer must be sent to address or P.O. Box specified on request. No other company address will be honored nor requests forwarded. (This is because most manufacturers use clearinghouses to process their forms. More about these later.).
- Offer void where restricted, taxed, licensed, or prohibited by law.
- Offer valid only to residents of the United States, District of Columbia, Puerto Rico, and U.S government installations (valid APO/FPO box numbers).
- Multiple, commercial, group, or organization requests will not be honored or acknowledged.
- Expiration date of offer is (__/__/__). Requests must be postmarked by that date. Most offers are good for six to eight months.
- Total refund claimed may be limited per address or name.

These same, recurring terms are specified in thousands of refund/rebate offers. Commit them to memory and they will ensure your regular flow of checks and coupons. Knowing them will make your research and gathering prossess easier since you will know what to look for 99 percent of the time.

Tips on Filling Out Forms and Sending Out Requests

Above all, fill out your forms *legibly* and *clearly*. If the clearinghouse workers, who process literally thousands of forms daily, can't read your name and address, they can't send you your money. It's as simple as that.

Make sure you get your request in the mail several days before the expiration date. I have never been able to figure out the relationship between when your letter goes in the mailbox and when it gets postmarked. It's one of the great mysteries of the postal department. I always make sure I have plenty of time to get that important postmark date.

Circle your purchase in red on your register receipt. That way the processors can't miss it and disqualify you.

Check to see that you have included *all* proofs of purchases required in the offer. This may be from one to three proofs, from the same or differing products. The offer may also specify purchase of a particular size, weight, or flavor of a product. In our experience, *sample* and *trial size* proofs of purchase are never accepted.

If the offer allows you to use substitution request forms in place of an original, fill one out on a blank piece of paper or index card, again legibly and neatly, giving all information as requested in the original. Or they may allow photocopies of an original request. If you need to add additional information or if there is not enough space on the form, use another piece of paper along with the original.

Also, attach your proof(s) of purchase to a separate piece of paper to avoid their getting lost if your envelope is opened by a mechanical device. Staple extra papers and POPs at the corners rather than using tape or paper clips. Mechanical, high-speed envelope openers are just like they sound, mechanical, not human. They can rip and destroy unfamiliar contents faster than you can lick a stamp. Only enclose one refund request per envelope, even if you are not limited to the number you can send for.

If more than two weeks go beyond the time suggested for delivery of your refund, send an inquiry to the original P.O. Box or address stated in the offer. (Keep a journal or ledger-type record of all entries sent and final dates for when you should receive your check or coupon.) The address is most likely that of a clearinghouse that processes requests for hundreds of product promotions. If you experience any problems or do not get your refund, the following are names of fulfillment houses used by major manufacturers:

NIELSON CLEARING HOUSE
Promotional Services
75 Tri-State International #400
Lincolnshire, IL 60069-4443
(800) 833-7096

CARLSON MARKETING
Consumer Service
5130 Industrial Blvd.
Maple Plain, MN 55359
(612) 479-4100

PROMOTIONAL FULFILLMENT CORPORATION
Consumer Service
PFC Plaza
Highway 67 North
Camanche, IA 52730
(319) 243-0100

YOUNG AMERICA CORPORATION
Consumer Service Department
717 Faxon Road
Young America, MN 55397
(612) 467-3366

FULFILLMENT SYSTEMS (FSI)
P.O. Box 4000
Monticello, MN 55362
(612) 295-2929

NATIONWIDE FULFILLMENT SYSTEMS
Customer Service
P. O. Box 500
Ridgely, MD 21660
(800) 223-1978

If you get into trading offers by joining a club or attending a convention, check all your trades to make sure they are valid in your area. Although most refund offers are for nationally distributed products, you might run across some products or services that are available only in certain locales or regions.

Refunding Clubs, Conventions, and Newsletters

Elaborate networks of refunding/couponing clubs and conventions exist for those who want to maximize their opportunities for profit through couponing and refunding. By joining a club, you can trade useless coupons and offers for those you can use as well as exchange information, systems, and techniques. By attending local, regional and national conventions, you can expand your contacts and share information with hundreds of enterprising folks just like you—interested in reaping the benefits of this occupation (at this level, couponing and refunding becomes an occupation, rather than a hobby). Often there are featured speakers who share valuable tips and their success stories.

Refund magazines and newsletters contain detailed information on current refund offers and extensive advertising sections for refunders interested in trading through the mail. (You can also trade with your friends and neighbors who refund.) These publications are packed with information about premiums, sweepstakes, and contests, cash-plus offers, cardboard backings, POPs, how to get additional forms, etc. Look for magazine and newspaper listings in your pennysaver bulletins, classified shopper weeklies, supermarket bulletin board, recycler newspaper, or Yellow Pages.

You can buy additional request forms through clubs and newsletters. Keep in mind, however, the cost of the form (usually around $.25), plus your postage and envelope must be worth sending for, since you will still have to spend money on mailing out your request, two more envelopes, and stamps. Add these up to see if they total more than your expected rebate.

The following is a list of publications that specialize in couponing and refunding. Bulletins list offers alphabetically, by brand, by expiration date, by no-form and form-required offers, or at random. However, prices are not guarantee of good quality. Ask for a sample copy (enclose a SASE) of each before deciding which one(s) you want to subscribe to.

MONEYTALK, P.O. Box 1677, Kingston, PA 18704. Published monthly. 1 issue: $2.50; 12 issues (1 year): $19.

NO FORM NEEDED ROUND-UP, P.O. Box 783, Republic, PA 15475 or R.D. 1, Box 16A-1, Hopwood, PA 15445. Published bimonthly; appproximately 40 pages. 1 issue: $2.50; 6 issues (1 year): $13.50.

REFUND EXPRESS, P.O. Box 1210, Monroe, GA 30655. Published monthly. 1 issue: $2.50.

REFUND WORLD, Box 16001, Philadelphia, PA 19114. (Took over Quick Silver and Quick Silver and Gold.) Published monthly. Approximately 40 pages; 350+ new refund offers each month. 1 issue: $1.75; 12 issues (1 year): $14.50.

REFUNDING MAKES CENTS, P.O. Box R, Farmington, UT 84025. Published monthly; 500+ new refund offers each month. 1 issue: $2; 12 issues (1 year): $18.

REFUNDING $ENSE BULLETIN, P.O. Box 458132, Cincinnati, OH 45225. 1 issue: $2.50.

REFUNDLE BUNDLE, P.O. Box 141, Centuck Station, Yonkers, NY 10710, (914) 472-2227. Published bimonthly. 1 issue: $2.50; 6 issues (1 year): $9; 12 issues (2 years): $14.87.

ROADRUNNER REFUNDER, 6535 West Ellis, Laveen, AZ 85339, (602) 237-4611. Published bimonthly. Approximately 50 pages; 300+ new refund offers each month. 1 issue: $2; 12 issues (1 year): $14.

RUBBISH TRADING, P.O. Box 278, Creswell, OR 97426. For sample issue, send a no-expiration-date coupon good for a free item.

TENNESSEE VALLEY REFUND BULLETIN, Route 2, Box 77, Thorn Hill, TN 3788-9419. 1 issue: $2.

For a free listing of refund bulletins belonging to the Best of Editors association of refund newletter editors, send a business-size SASE to: BEST OF EDITORS, P.O. Box 26, Thorn Hill, TN 37881-9419.

Examples of Supermarket and Drug Store Refund Offers

Note: In most cases below, wording has been taken directly off original request forms; nearly every offer listed requires an original, dated cash register receipt with purchase circled; trial sizes of products are not accepted; lined UPC code or symbol is the same as proof-of-purchase.

Film, Light Bulbs and Batteries. A listing appears on the following page for refunds on these particular items.

- $3 refund offer with UPC symbols from two GE Soft-White products and one cash register receipt from any milk purchase.

- $1 refund offer with UPC symbol from any GE Battery package, AAA, AA, C, D, 9 volt.
- $2 off mail-in rebate for next photofinishing order with purchase of any three Kodak video cassettes.
- $1 cash back by mail with proof-of-purchase symbol(s) from one or more packages (any size) totaling four (4) or more Eveready Classic brand batteries.
- $4 rebate with proof-of-purchase seals from product boxes of three packs of Polaroid film, $2 rebate with proof-of-purchase seals from boxes of two packs of Polaroid film; $10 rebate with proof of purchase from Polaroid Impulse FF camera, and $20 rebate with proof-of-purchase from Polaroid Impulse AF camera.
- $1 cash refund by mail *and* $1 donation to help kids at participating Hospitals for Children (as a sponsor of Children's Miracle Network) with proofs of purchase from any two packages (any size) or one Super Pack of Eveready Super Heavy Duty batteries.

Liquor. Refund offers on liquor and spirits are listed on the following page. In our state, California, these are quite common. A few years ago, however, these types of offers were rare, since many state laws prohibited promotional incentives for alcoholic beverages. Now you can find them in several states and regions of the United States, especially since alcohol consumption has been decreasing steadily each year and beer and wine and liquor manufacturers are in heavy competition for shrinking consumer dollars.

These offers are generally for several dollars or more, making them especially valuable. Of course, your original purchase is going to cost more than a normal supermarket item. They also usually expire within three months. You can find many liquor offers around the holidays, October through December. Cooking and recipe booklets are often offered free with the rebate (or for a small postage and handling charge).

Look for offers on liquor store, supermarket, and drugstore shelves next to the products and on bulletin board displays as tear-off pads. With the cost of major brands today, these mail-in offers represent some of the biggest savings in household goods.

- $4 tax deduction rebate with UPC code from one I.75L bottle of Gordon's Vodka; $8 rebate with UPC codes from Gordon's Vodka, Gordon's Gin, or George Dickel Old Charter; $12 rebate with UPC codes from one bottle of Gordon's Vodka, one bottle of Gordon's Gin and one bottle of George Dickel Old Charter.
- $1.50 "holiday" refund from Gordon's Vodka, 1.75L or one liter bottle of Gordon's Vodka.
- $2 refund with UPC code from one liter bottle of Canadian Club; $3 refund with UPC code from one 1.75L bottle of Canadian Club.
- $2 refund with UPC symbol from one 1.75L bottle of Seagram's 7 Crown.

Medicines, Vitamins and Beauty Products. Below is a listing of refunds for these items.

- $1 with entire back panel with UPC symbol from one package of any Oral-B Art or Sport series toothbrush.
- $1 refund offer with three (3) proof-of-purchase points from packages of Kleenex Huggies diapers.
- $2 rebate with order number cut from the tuck-in flaps of two B-D Alcohol Swabs box tops.
- $1 cash rebate with UPC symbol from Unisol4 saline solution (for contact lens wearers); $1 cash rebate with UPC symbol from Pliagel cleaning solution for contact lenses.

- $1.50 refund on Motrin IB pain reliever with entire carton of any Motrin IB tablet or caplet product.
- $1 cash rebate with one UPC code from Coriciden or Coriciden "D" decongestant tablets.
- $4 refund check by mail with two UPC codes from any variety or size of One-A-Day, Flintstones, or Bugs Bunny vitamins; or $1.50 refund check by mail with one UPC code from either One-A-Day Flintstones, or Bugs Bunny vitamins.
- $2 cash refund offer with one plastic hinge or the punch-out disc from any bottle of Agree shampoo or conditioner.
- $2 refund check by mail with UPC code from any size of either Alka-Seltzer Plus Cold Medicine or Alka-Seltzer Plus Night-Time Cold Medicine.
- $2 refund offer with UPC code from one Revlon Colorsilk or Frost & Glow box.
- $1 refund offer by mail from any Di-Gel product with proof of purchase (UPC code on back of box or the whole printed neckband). Also receive one coupon by mail good on one free package of Di-Gel with proofs of purchase from any two Di-Gel products.
- 1/2 price refund mail-in with proof of purchase (inner pull top lid of powders or UPC bar code from tablets/wafers) from any Fiberall product.
- $1.25 cash refund with UPC/Proof of purchase seal from one package of Ascriptin, Ascriptin A/D, or Extra Strength Ascriptin pain relief medicine (75 count or larger).
- $1 refund check for purchasing Vicks Throat Drops or Victors Cough Drops with UPC symbol(s) from: one Vicks Throat Drops bag, one Victors Cough Drops bag, two Vicks Throat Drops boxes, or two Victors Cough Drops boxes.

Chapter 2

- $1.50 refund check with two UPC symbols from any size Daycare and NyQuil (one each) cold medicine.
- $1 refund by mail offer with UPC symbol from the outer carton of any size Lotrimin AF cure for athlete's foot.
- $2 cash by mail from Sunkist Vitamin C.
- $5 rebate by mail with UPC code from package back of Eyegel eye moisturizer.
- $1 cash rebate by mail with UPC code from the bottom of one carton (any size) of Progaine shampoo.
- $1 cash refund by mail with one Flicker (women's shaver) proof of purchase (the word "Flicker" from the front of the package).
- $1.50 in cash refund or $2 in coupons (four $.50 coupons each good on one box of Tampax tampons 40s or 24s) with UPC symbol from bottom panel of Tampax tampons 10s package.
- $4 cash refund by mail with proof of purchase (UPC symbol) from any two Correctol 60s or 90s laxative tablets.
- Gift certificate (up to $1.39 value) for a free Ultra Rich shampoo or conditioner with cap hinges off any two Ultra Rich products.
- $1 cash refund with one, two or three proofs of purchase from Personna Twin Blade disposable 10s, 3s, 5s, or Lady Personna disposable shaving blades.
- $2 refund by mail with plastic overwrap (on liquid products) or UPC bar code (from tablets carton) from any two Kaopectate products for relief from diarrhea and cramping.
- Receive by mail two free coupons, each good for a free two-liter bottle of Pepsi or Diet Pepsi with three proofs of purchase—one from Band-Aid Brand Adhesive Bandages

and any two other Band-Aid or Johnson & Johnson products listed in mail-in certificate.

Food and Miscellaneous. A listing of food and miscellaneous refunds are listed below.

- $1 coupon refund offer with two Egg Beaters seals. Receive coupon by mail good on one package of Egg Beaters (cholesterol-free real egg product).
- Coupon for one free package of Pillsbury Crescent Dinner Rolls with UPC symbols from three packages of Pillsbury Crescent Dinner Rolls.
- Free Bugs Bunny plush toy with four proofs of purchase from any four Colgate Palmolive products listed in offer (including soap, toothbrushes, toothpaste, deodorant, detergent). (Enclose $1.50 for postage and handling.) Or Colgate will donate the plush toy to a Starlight child.
- $1.50 refund by mail with proof of purchase on Prestone Anti Freeze/Coolant, one-gallon size and imprinted foil seal from the mouth of Prestone Anti Freeze/Coolant. $3 refund on two-gallon purchase.
- $3.50 coupon offer (includes several $.50 coupons) with UPC code cut from back label of any PeggyJane's Salad Dressing. Receive coupons by mail; good for PeggyJane and Knott's Berry Farm products.
- $1 coupon refund offer on next purchase of coffee with UPC code from two 16 oz. or larger Cremora or Cremora Lite (nondairy creamer) labels.
- Receive by mail: $10 value booklet of coupons, recipe book mail-in certificates, and Eagle brand dessert recipes with two Eagle brand condensed milk labels and one proof of purchase from any store brand vanilla extract, cream cheese, flour, or pie filling.

- Free bread offer (coupon valued up to $.99) with three proofs of purchase (UPC code) from one package of Bordon Cheese, one Hillshire Farm Deli Select meat, and one loaf of bread.
- $1 refund by mail with one proof-of-purchase symbol from inside any 12 or 14.4 oz. can of Beer Nuts brand Snacks Peanuts or two UPC proof-of-purchase symbols from back of 5.5 oz. peanuts bag, 3 oz. cashews bag, or 4.1 oz. almonds bag.
- $1.50 worth of coupons good for $.50 off any brand of chicken with purchase of Shake 'n Bake. Receive coupons with mail in of one UPC Symbol from any variety or size of Shake 'n Bake Seasoning and Coating Mixture.
- $2 refund by mail with UPC code from any Slim-Fast, Ultra Slim-Fast package.

ALTERNATIVES TO SAVING AT THE SUPERMARKET

Your neighborhood supermarket is probably the most convenient place for you to shop, if not always the most reasonable. However, in recent years, establishments that specialize in low-priced products, such as warehouse stores, discount stores, thrift shops, co-ops, manufacturers' outlets, farmers' markets, etc. have been creeping closer and closer to the suburbs and popular metropolitan shopping areas. No longer selling only to strictly limited "business" or "membership" populations, most of these organizations either welcome the public or have membership requirements flexible enough that nearly anyone can meet them.

In order to feed the growing hunger of Americans for savings on every kind of consumable food and product (even at the cost of buying in huge quantities or bulk packaging), these types of stores have enjoyed a tremendous boom over the past decade.

Many have several hundred outlets in every region of the country. And with the current uncertain economic outlook, it looks as if their growth will continue throughout the 1990s.

In this chapter we will explain alternatives to the supermarket that offer additional savings to you. We've purposely omitted those alternatives that will end up costing you more money in the long run, although their selection and products may be of equal or even superior quality. These include convenience stores, specialty stores, wine, cheese and pasta stores, neighborhood stores, ethnic food stores, and the current trend in "gourmet" shops and supermarkets.

Still, your supermarket should not be overlooked for its advantages of convenience, reasonable pricing, and variety. In fact, by utilizing our methods of couponing, refunding and shopping for products on sale, you many never need to shop anywhere else for food and household goods. In fact, one corner of most supermarkets that is often ignored by shoppers is the "day-old" rack of fruits, vegetables, and other perishables. If you like to give your family fresh produce, but hate to pay high prices due to strikes, droughts, floods, freezes, etc., check out the "sale" rack next to the produce section and take home a selection of perfectly good, fresh produce. If cooked and served right away, nearly all of these products are just as nutritious and tasty as those displayed in stacks of neat and tidy rows.

You should also check prices and quality of supermarket brand products. Many of us already know that generic products and "knock offs" can be as good or in some cases, better than the original "brand name" or "designer" products. This goes for household goods and food as well as drugs, clothing, and appliances. Store brands are always cheaper, because they don't have the huge advertising and promotional dollars behind them that keep prices high. However, they often come from the same processing plants, factories, canneries, and manufacturers as name brand goods. Just the label and the price are different. Next time you go to buy a name-brand product, buy one of the store-brand items next to it. Compare the two at home (with your family as taste testers), and you may end up saving considerably on future shopping trips.

Finally, nonfood items such as paper towels, toilet paper, trashbags, picnic supplies, plastic utensils, dishwasher and laundry detergents, napkins, shampoos and conditioners, toothpaste, and tissues have very high mark-ups at the retail supermarket level. If you can purchase these items on sale and in conjunction with double coupons, they *can* be a good buy. Otherwise you will probably do much better buying in bulk or multi-packed quantities from discount and warehouse stores. If you can find the space to store these products (a garage or basement will do nicely) you will save on them in the long run.

Warehouse Shopping Clubs

Variously called "wholesale clubs," "warehouse clubs," "membership discount stores," "wholesale cash-and-carry warehouses," and "wholesale centers," these huge establishments represent a type of wholesaling that is growing rapidly in metropolitan areas around the country. Some specialize in a specific type of product, such as office supplies, sporting goods, hardware, housewares and garden products, children's clothes and accessories, while others carry a huge assortment of products from foodstuffs, clothing, liquor and cigarettes, tapes and CDs, to appliances and electronic equipment. Products are often bundled in groups or come only in bulk and extra-large sizes.

The idea behind most of these centers is to provide merchandise at or near wholesale prices to two categories of private customers: (1) small businesses—restaurants, small retailers, service firms, and professionals; and (2) individual consumers who work for or are members of a loosely "qualified" group, such as a credit union, or government employees.

These are strictly cash-and-carry operations: no-fuss, no-frills with a minimum of service and amenities. There are no fancy displays, music, or attractive decorations to lure the customers. Centers are typically self-service warehouses of 100,000 feet or more.

Membership policies vary. Some charge no fee but require members to offer proof of business, such as a license or business card. Some charge members an annual fee ($25 or less) while others do not charge individual members, but add a small percentage (5%) to their total bill. All require you show a membership card before entering and/or when paying.

While you may not see the normal wide choice of brands within a certain product category, you generally have one or two major brands to choose from. Also, items may vary from week to week, depending on type of "buy" the operators have made with manufacturers.

The following is a list of major chain wholesale clubs in the United States. Call to find locations in your area.

BJ'S WHOLESALE CLUB, INC.
(800) BJS-CLUB; in Massachusetts (800) 257-7100. Locations in Connecticut, Delaware, Illinois, Maine, New Hampshire, New Jersey, New York, Ohio, and Rhode Island.

COSTCO WHOLESALE
(206) 828-8100. Locations in Alaska, California, Florida, Nevada, Oregon, Utah, Washington, and Canada.

PACE MEMBERSHIP WAREHOUSE, INC.
(303) 843-8000. Locations in California, Colorado, Connecticut, Florida, Iowa, Kentucky, Maryland, Michigan, Nebraska, New Jersey, New York, North Carolina, Ohio, Pennsylvania, Rhode Island and Washington, D.C.

PRICE CLUB
(619) 581-4728. Locations in Arizona, Connecticut, Maryland, New Jersey, New York, Virginia, New Mexico, and throughout California. Locations also in Canada.

PRICE SAVERS WHOLESALE WAREHOUSE
(801) 974-0220. Locations in Alaska, Arizona, California, Kentucky, Ohio, Utah, and Washington.

SAM'S WHOLESALE CLUB
(501) 273-6839. Locations in Alabama, Arkansas, Colorado, Florida, Georgia, Illinois, Indiana, Kansas, Kentucky, Louisiana, Minnesota, Mississippi, Missouri, Nebraska, New Jersey, New York, North Carolina, North Dakota, Ohio, Oklahoma, Pennsylvania, Tennessee, Texas, South Carolina, South Dakota, Virginia, Wisconsin, and West Virginia.

WAREHOUSE CLUB, INC.
(708) 647-6801. Locations in Illinois, Michigan, Ohio, and Pennsylvania.

Thrift Stores

These are not the kind of "thrift store" that carry used clothing, books, toys, and household goods that people no longer have use for. These are generally bakery outlets that offer day-old breads, pastries, muffins, bagels, cookies, buns, and doughnuts. Many of them carry the products of only one brand. Prices are often 30 to 50 percent less than retail, and generally speaking, most of us can barely discern between a fresh and a day-old loaf of wheat-berry or French bread. The following is a list of thrift stores operated by national bakeries and independent suppliers.

ARNOLD'S BAKERY THRIFT STORES
Carries Arnold's day-old bread, cakes, and cookies. Locations in South Carolina, Massachusetts, New Jersey, New York, and Pennsylvania.

ENTENMANN'S BAKERY OUTLETS
Fresh and day-old bakery goods. Locations in Maryland, Ohio, Florida, Pennsylvania, New York, New Jersey, and Connecticut.

PEPPERIDGE FARM THRIFT STORES
Features day-old breads, rolls and frozen products. Located in Connecticut, Massachusetts, New Jersey, New York, Pennsylvania, and Georgia.

SUNBEAM BREAD AND CAKE THRIFT STORES
Day-old breads and cakes. Locations in North Carolina, Massachusetts, and Connecticut.

WONDER BREAD/HOSTESS CAKES BAKERY THRIFT SHOPS
Day-old bread and cakes. Locations in Washington, D.C., Virginia, Maryland North Carolina, Pennsylvania, New York, New Jersey, Rhode Island, New Hampshire, Massachusetts, Maine, and California.

OROWEAT THRIFT STORES
Day-old bread and cakes. Locations in California, Colorado, Texas, Oregon, and Washington.

Discount Stores

Discount stores for food and other products generally offer lower overall prices and a limited choice of brands. If you like having several manufacturers' products to choose from, then you might be better off shopping at one or two of your local supermarkets and having the option of buying your favorite products on sale or at the regular price.

Outlet Stores

These are stores that carry one brand of product that is usually canned, packaged, milled, boxed, or otherwise processed at the same site as goods being shipped to retailers. An outlet store carrying overruns or products with slight defects will have basically same products you see on your grocery shelves, but for much less than you would normally pay. These include dairies, chicken farms, egg farms, canneries, etc.

The recent wave of manufacturers' outlets for everything from designer clothes to cookware, linens, china, utensils, outerwear, sporting goods, shoes, children's clothing, etc., has caught on with consumers in the latest wave of wanting to get "more for less" Outlet malls have sprung up throughout the country, in areas adjacent to major ski resorts, recreational attractions, and tourist areas, as well as major population centers.

Make sure you are familiar with the brand's retail prices before you buy merchandise in an outlet store. Although most "true" outlets offer savings from 20–60 percent below retail, some offer no better savings than general department or specialty stores during their regular sales. Often your local department store is more convenient and will have a more flexible return/credit policy.

Superstores

These are basically, giant supermarkets that have expanded services such as optical centers, travel services, camera corners, small appliance centers and cafe-type restaurants. Prices are competitive with regular supermarkets but generally not as low as warehouse stores. A wider range of selection and services is their main draw.

Farmer's Markets and Flower Marts

If you can't go directly to the source for the freshest fruits and vegetables, then why not bring the source to you? This is happening in urban and suburban communities all over the country where growers can bring fresh food and sell directly to consumers. Many people, dissatisfied with the quality of produce in their markets, are finding this is the easiest and most successful way to get the best possible produce.

Americans have been complaining for years that fruits and vegetables just don't taste like they used to. And they don't. With modern agricultural methods of growing and harvesting, geared towards maximum efficiency, production and profit, a good portion of our produce arrives at the market as oversized, underripe, tasteless testaments to the wonders of agricultural science. It may look prettier each year, but what you see is not as good as what you get.

Enter Farmer's Markets. These are usually supported by local or state governments or by nonprofit organizations. They are set up to support local and family farms, to revitalize downtown areas, and to bring fresh, inexpensive food to urban residents.

In Oakland, several thousand Bay Area cooks and shoppers gather each year for an annual Tasting of Summer Produce, where nearly 100 growers display dozens of varieties of fruits and vegetables for sampling, comparing, and purchasing. Thousands more shoppers meet weekly at various farmers' markets in New York City, Los Angeles, Decatur, Seattle, Oakland, and dozens of communities in between to take advantage of this age-old event. Some have even become popular as social gatherings, with shoppers meeting and exchanging news and gossip from the past week. More importantly, however, quality is measurably higher. Choices range from the exotic to the everyday "garden variety," and prices are lower, up to 40 percent lower, coming direct from the source.

Fresh flowers and herbs are often available, in addition to produce. Since prices for these products have risen substantially in recent years, it is a welcome change to buy beautiful fresh flowers and "just picked" herbs at reasonable prices. Of course, if you want to get the absolute lowest prices on flowers, you can go to your community's flower market—which is usually open between 2:00 A.M. and 5:00 A.M.

Also, consider looking into local self-serve orchards for getting fresh produce. Apple, cherry, and berry orchards all over the Northeast and West invite the public to come and pick produce, selling it by the pound or bushel. Some orange growers will allow the public to pick their juicy fruits in bountiful years.

Roadside fruit stands dot the agricultural regions of our country. These local farmers sell "picked that day" fruits and vegetables that have been grown within a stone's throw of the stand. You can bet they taste as good as they look. And as an additional bonus, the prices are again far below retail since you are buying directly from the source.

Barter in the 1990s:
Co-ops, Buying Clubs, Networks, and Exchanges

A cooperative (co-op) is an organization owned and run by members in a democratic fashion for the purpose of providing needed goods and services at the lowest possible prices. Primarily nonprofit, exchanges between members are seen as mutually advantageous. Co-ops can serve its members only or it can serve an entire community.

Consumer co-ops and buying clubs sprang up in America during the mid-1800s and flourished until World War II. The war and postwar boom economy provided nearly 100 percent employment and eventually caused a steady decline and interest in cooperative membership. In the 1960s, experiments in alternative lifestyles and a desire to return to a more "self-reliant" way of life, revived the cooperative movement.

Today's extended unstable economic environment (heldover from the 1980s) has fostered a sizable, growing community committed to the principles of cooperative living and working.

There are several kinds of consumer cooperatives, including the kind with which most of us are familiar, food co-ops. In addition, there are:

- Food-buying clubs where community people gather together with their orders for cheese, grains, vegetables, etc.
- Small co-op stores that have expanded the buying club concept into a storefront business.
- Co-ops for getting heat and gas.

- Housing cooperatives where groups of people get together to build, buy, or rehabilitate housing for its members and possibly others
- Member discount co-ops, where members receive substantial discounts on their purchases immediately rather than waiting until the end of the year to split up their savings. Nonmembers may be able to shop at the co-op, but they do not receive the discount that members do.

Consumer co-ops exist for types of goods and services that can be shared, exchanged, or traded. They can be very small neighborhood co-ops with less than a dozen members sharing baby-sitting, marketing, and car-pooling, or they can be extremely large, national organizations like Recreational Equipment Incorporated (REI), where over 350,000 members share discounts on quality recreational equipment and sporting goods.

Food-buying coops utilize their members for ordering, telephoning, receiving, picking up, repackaging, shelf stocking, and basically all labor-intensive jobs that are entailed in running a food business. By eliminating brokers and middlemen, members can reap from 15 to 50 percent savings on most items. The greatest savings are generally on produce and perishable goods purchased directly from growers. Packaged goods, because of their longer shelf life, usually have a lower mark-up in the stores, and therefore represent somewhat lower savings in co-ops. However, you can realize an additional discount since you can often buy goods in larger quantities at co-ops than at the retail level.

There is also the added benefit of buying food in unprocessed bulk form rather than packaged, processed, and chock-full of additives. With today's concerns about cholesterol levels, fat content, high blood pressure, heart disease, and cancer-causing chemical additives, many people prefer to shop at cooperatives offering food in the natural (and often organic) state.

Networks or exchanges work similarly to co-ops, except that they deal in exchanging information rather than actual goods and services. Today, more than 400 bartering clubs with about 175,000 business members operate in the United States. Bartering networks link people together who otherwise would never meet.

There are networks for aiding seniors and low-income groups with housing, food, and medical care and networks for helping members of a specific age group or expertise find employment or exchange their skills. There are educational and learning networks for parents, professionals, and enthusiasts. There are business networks for meeting others in your profession (or a profession you would *like* to join) and social networks for folks who are single or divorced. There are several networks just for women re-entering the work force, women who are single mothers, women caretakers of aging parents, and widows.

And there are organizations whose members will freely share a wide variety of specialized skills with other members without charge or the need to balance out their services with a credit-like system. One such organization in Los Angeles is called FREE FOR ALL. Members pay a modest one-time registration fee. After that they can arrange trades from a pool of services including accounting, auto repair, wardrobe consultation, prenatal instruction, legal advice, medical advice, household repair, and a variety of useful merchandise. For more information about this organization call: (818) 788-SAVE.

Since the early 1960s, when the first barter club was formed, hundreds of clubs and trade exchanges have emerged as clearinghouses for individuals or businesses with something to trade. However, before joining any cooperative, network, exchange or barter club, it's a good idea to check them out thoroughly before putting any money down. Many people do not fully understand the systems and terms involved in these types of organizations, and not all organizations are fiscally sound or competently managed. The following is a list of sources that will help educate you and lead you toward a rewarding bartering experience:

*THE COOPERATIVE LEAGUE OF THE U.S.A. (CLUSA)
a.k.a. NATIONAL CO-OPERATIVE BUSINESS
ASSOCIATION (NCBA)*
1401 New York Ave. NW, Suite 1100
Washington, D.C. 20005
(202) 638-6222
For $4.95 you can send for their *Finding Co-ops Directory and Reference*. They also have an extensive publications catalog with sources on all aspects of cooperatives.

THE NATIONAL ASSOCIATION OF NEIGHBORHOODS
1651 Fuller Street NW
Washington, D.C. 20009
(202) 332-7766
This association supports neighborhood involvement in self-help enterprises and service delivery projects.

NORTH AMERICAN STUDENTS OF COOPERATION (NASCO)
Box 7715
Ann Arbor, MI 48107
(313) 663-0889
Write them for their free bi-annual listing of student co-ops in the United States "Guide to Campus Cooperatives," including student-housing, retail, dining, childcare, and food co-ops.

PEOPLE'S YELLOW PAGES
(Look them up in your phone book, at your library, in alternative book stores and natural/health food stores.)

These exist in several cities as directories listing various resources for trading and exchanging goods and services of all kinds. They're kind of a word-of-mouth grapevine that has been set to paper.

BARTER NEWS
P.O.Box 3024
Mission Viejo, CA 92690
(714) 495-6529
Barter News reports on the changes and evaluation of barter and shows potential barterers how to profitably use barter systems. Hundereds of offerings, one-year subscription (4 issues): $40.

THE INTERNATIONAL RECIPROCAL TRADE ASSOCIATION
 (formerly International Association of Trade Exchanges)
5152 Woodmere Lane
Alexandria, VA 22311
(703) 379-2838

DO IT YOURSELF AND SAVE

If you've ever tasted a juicy, red tomato that has been allowed to ripen on the vine, you know just how delectable home-grown fruits and vegetables can be. No store-bought tomato can compare to that sweet, full-flavored vegetables. Yet, although few of us would have trouble finding a sunny corner in which to grow a plant or two, many don't even think to do it.

This is a real shame. One way to cut your food bill in the produce section is by starting a small home garden. You get to choose what you grow (subject to space and climate limitations, of course), you avoid the chemicals that are often used on commercially-grown produce, and you and your family get to watch the miracle of nature as seedlings turn into mature plants.

If you are lucky enough to have a yard, you may be able to grow most of the vegetables your family needs, for a lot less money than you'd pay at the supermarket. A five foot by five foot garden can yield 200 tomatoes, 40 or 50 beets, over 100 carrots, all the lettuce you can eat, and more. That's at least 200 pounds of vegetables, when properly handled. A ten foot by ten foot garden can yield 1,000 pounds—enough to keep a family of four in veggies through the growing season.

Even those who live in apartments can become "home gardeners" by placing large flowerpots or flowerboxes on a balcony or in a sunny corner of your living room. Four tomato plants and a dozen or so of leaf lettuce will provide as many salads as the average family can eat, and probably more. And the time and effort they require are minimal—just some watering, fertilizing, and tender loving care. If you start with sterile soil and keep the plants indoors, you won't need to weed the plants or worry about pests or the weather, either.

The key to successful home gardening, as anyone who has tried it will tell you, is to learn as much as possible before you get started. Head over to your local library for books on the subject. Or ask the experts at your neighborhood nursery. Both will help you figure out what you should plant based on your area's climate, how much room—and time—you can spare, and what your family will actually eat. You can get advice on soil preparation, spacing of plants, when planting should begin, troubleshooting, and more.

One excellent resource for home gardeners is *The Backyard Vegetable Factory: Super Yields from Small Spaces,* by Duane Newcomb (Rodale, PA: Rodale Press, 1988). By using "super soil," dynamic plant groupings, and unconventional spacing, this book shows you how to construct a miniature, interactive vegetable garden that will outproduce most traditional gardens.

With even a few plants, you'll harvest enough to put a dent in your produce bill, while serving your family wholesome, more flavorful fruits and vegetables. But perhaps best of all, gardening is fun!

MAKE YOUR OWN CONVENIENCE FOODS

Money and time are probably the two scarcest commodities these days. Most families today rely on two salaries to get by, meaning that the full-time homemaker, who has time to cook meals from scratch, is becoming less and less common. Unfortunately, saving money and saving time are two goals that are often at odds with each other.

As a result, we often find ourselves turning to pre-packaged convenience foods such as T.V. dinners and boxed mixes. These time-savers, though easy, are much more expensive than their homemade equivalents. They are also likely to be loaded with salt, sugar, fats, and chemical additives that make them less than ideal for everyday use.

I'm not suggesting that you go back to making everything from scratch. But there are ways for you to cut back on your use of those overpriced, supermarket convenience foods and still spend a lot less time in the kitchen. How? Make your own.

When I am shortest on time, I find that the easiest way to prepare dinner is to reach into my freezer for a few frozen dinners to throw in the microwave. At around $3 for a box from the supermarket that contains barely enough for one person, this would be a relatively expensive way to feed my family. But I don't buy these meals at the supermarket.

Instead, I prepare them myself every time we have leftovers. I simply fill a freezer-to-microwave safe plate or container with single-serving portions of the leftovers, cover it, label it with the date and contents, and pop it into the freezer for future use. When I need a fast, healthy meal, I just pop it into the microwave, and it's ready to serve.

Making your own frozen dinners from leftovers takes only seconds. You've already done the cooking, so the only time you spend is in preparing the plates. And the dinners keep for weeks in the freezer, so you can rotate the meals for added variety.

Don't limit yourself to dinner, either. One of my favorite time-savers is to make extra pancakes on a lazy weekend morning, tightly wrap the stacks in plastic, and refrigerate them. During the week, when I might not otherwise have time to make anything but cold cereal, I can serve hot, homemade pancakes for breakfast.

This technique is so economical, I have started to plan my leftovers. If the dish I'm making for dinner is one that is time consuming but freezes well, such as a stew, I simply double the recipe. I then freeze half for later use. A few days (or weeks) later, when I've had a particularly hard day and can't bear the thought of cooking, all I have to do is heat it up!

In fact, many of the packaged convenience foods that we all take for granted as a necessary part of modern life can be prepared wholesomely and economically at home and then stored for later use. Helen Witty and Elizabeth Schneider Colchie have written a book that is packed with how-to's for hundreds of foods—convenience and otherwise—that you may never have thought of making at home. *Better Than Store-Bought* (New York: Harper & Row, 1979) offers recipes for such things as pancake and biscuit mixes, chicken boullion, hot fudge sauce, and yogurt. Still more money-saving recipes can be found in *Cheaper and Better* by Nancy Birnes (New York: Harper & Row, 1987). This book even provides a breakdown of exactly how much you will save with each recipe.

Not only are these homemade convenience foods generally much less expensive than their store-bought equivalents, but they are also a lot healthier for you. Prepared in advance and stored until you need them, they can be wonderful time-savers, too.

ALTERNATIVES TO STORE-BOUGHT BABY FOOD

One more tip: Breastfeeding your newborn can save you a bundle on formula, bottles amd sterilizing equipment. A new baby can drink up to two quarts of formula a day. At that rate, your monthly bill for ready-to-use formula alone may exceed $120. Even if you buy the concentrated formula that must be mixed with water before use, that monthly bill may reach $50. Add to that the cost of bottles and the effort spent sterilizing and filling them, and your potential savings in both time and money are substantial.

In addition to the cost savings, the superior nutritional value of breastmilk over formula will keep you and your baby happy until he or she is ready for more substantial fare. For more information, La Leché League International's *The Womanly Art of Breastfeeding* 3rd edition (New York: New American Library, 1990) is very informative.

It always amazes me how expensive those little supermarket jars of baby food are. Containing nothing but plain fruits, vegetables, or meats, and often thinned with water, they cost several times what the adult versions do. Why? Experts say that the packaging is the culprit. The cost to the company of the ingredients is minimal compared to the cost of those cute little serving-size jars.

What is even more amazing is that it doesn't occur to many parents that there is an alternative. Perhaps the simplest way to save money is to pass up the jars in the baby-food section in favor of larger jars in the regular section of the market. Applesauce, for instance, is just as healthy for your baby when spooned from a sixteen ounce jar as it is from a two-and-a-half ounce one, and the larger jar is much healthier for your pocketbook. A blender or a food processor will even enable you to make your own vegetable purees from cooked fresh, frozen, or low-salt canned carrots, peas, green beans, and more.

To provide your baby with the most varied diet from these homemade baby foods, and to get the biggest savings, you may want to make a one-time investment in a set of serving-size plastic containers. Or try freezing the purees in ice cube trays, then transferring the cubes to a plastic bag when they're frozen. This way you can take advantage of supermarket specials and coupon savings on adult-size packages of vegetables and fruits by stocking up and preparing your baby's purees in large batches. Not only will you save more, you will be able to keep a great selection of healthy, inexpensive, easily prepared foods on hand in your freezer, ready to defrost and serve to your little one.

SAVE ON DINING OUT AND EAT LIKE A KING

Everything I've told you so far can add up to more savings than you have ver imagined for all the thousands of shopping trips you'll be taking in your lifetime. But we all like an occasional change of scenery and relief from preparing meals and cleaning up. Treating yourself to a restaurant is the way to do it. The only problem is that restaurants are a lot worse than grocery stores when it comes to making dollars disappear.

Though every city has a variety of restaurants from which to choose, if you want something better than a fast-food chicken, taco, or hamburger drive-through, it's going to cost plenty. Even coffee-shop type chain restaurants, whose food is often not much better than fast-food fare (except that it's served on a *real* plate by a *real* waitress), can end up costing $30 to $50 for a family of four, including food, drinks, and service. A mid-priced "nice" restaurant can cost twice that amount. And fancy "special occasion" restaurants? Those are best left for "special occasions"—or when someone else is paying.

However, there are ways you *can* eat at restaurants cheaply or even for free, if you know how.

Make The Most of "Happy Hours"

What if you could patronize those "nice" restaurants and even the "special occasion" ones and get your fill of all the gourmet goodies you can eat for free? Not only is this possible, but many restaurants offer, advertise and encourage it.

This phenomenon, often called the "Happy Hour," usually lasts from around 4 to 6:30 P.M. and attracts people on their way home from work. However, now families with children are taking advantage of these feasts and eating for free.

One or more tables filled with hot and cold hors d'oeuvres are set up free to happy-hour customers. You can fill your plate as many times as you wish. They expect you to order a drink, but that can be any soft drink, mineral water, or fruit juice you might want to nurse for the next hour. (Be aware that underage children may not be allowed in the restaurant's bar area.) In the meantime, you can chow down on a variety of filling, delicious goodies that would take a lot of time and trouble to prepare at home.

This free food is the same quality that others pay for later, and provides you with a variety that is not only filling, but as satisfying as a full dinner. And it's usually a lot more fun!

Different kinds of restaurants advertise "happy hours." New restaurants, anxious to attract customers, will display large, outdoor banners announcing their "Get Acquainted Happy Hour." Established restaurants as well, whose business is slow during the early evening, may have a daily happy hour until business picks up around dinnertime. Some advertise in the local newspapers to bring in people from the neighborhood.

Mexican restaurants, especially, are famous for their elaborate happy-hour buffets. In addition, we've seen Chinese, German, Irish, and continental restaurants provide free gourmet buffets. Even the finest restaurants use this method to attract new customers when they first open. The offerings at these establishments are superb.

Other places with free feasts include restaurants located in large downtown office buildings or "gourmet" restaurants in large hotels. By offering a happy hour with free food, they can keep tenants and hotel guests "in-house" longer, in hopes that they will stay for a full dinner after Happy-hour cocktails. But we know better. Get the free food and split. For the price of a soda or cocktail, you can have your dinner, for free!

Early Birds Get the Deals

Another way to cut the cost of eating out is by taking advantage of early-bird specials. Restaurants don't make money when no one's eating in them. Between lunch and dinner, business drops dramatically—which is why some even close for several hours in the mid-afternoon. Restaurants that do stay open often use early-bird specials to help bring in customers during these otherwise slow hours. On the theory that *any* customers are better than *no* customers, they are likely to offer substantial discounts to those who are willing to eat during this off-peak period.

The early-bird specials offer the same food you'd normally get at the restaurant, but for a lot less money. Often they include not only an entree, but a beverage and a dessert, too—for less than you'd expect to spend for the entree alone. It's like getting a discount on the main course, and having the restaurant throw in your drink and dessert for free!

Early-bird dinner specials are usually available in the late afternoon to early evening hours, from around 3 to 6 P.M. Some restaurants, such as the INTERNATIONAL HOUSE OF PANCAKES, offer early-bird breakfast deals, as well. If you don't mind eating early, you can save a bundle—and not have to do the dishes.

These great deals are sometimes advertised in your local newspaper's food or entertainment section. But often they aren't advertised at all, except to their regular customers, who will find an insert in the regular menu or a listing of early-bird specials placed on their table. If you are not sure whether your favorite restaurants offer early-bird specials, try calling them. You'll be surprised at the deals you can get for eating a bit earlier.

Bring a Friend and Save

If you like to treat yourself to a meal out now and then but can't always make it during early-bird hours, you can still put a big dent in that end-of-meal check without sacrificing good food. Many restaurants offer special "2-for-1" deals to entice customers to try their establishments. You order two meals at regular menu prices, and the less expensive one is free! You get to go out to a nice restaurant, enjoy dinner with someone special, and get a meal for free.

Many different kinds of restaurants make 2-for-1 offers, from pancake houses to hamburger places, fine French bistros to trendy hot spots. The restaurants hope that once you've eaten there, you'll come back again and pay full price—so even if they lose money on your first visit, they'll make it up when you return. They may try to pressure you into padding your bill with extra salads, desserts, or high mark-up drinks. Don't fall for the waiter's sales pitch unless these are items you really want. Remember, you are only taking advantage of an offer the restaurant voluntarily made; you are there for a free meal.

With so many 2-for-1 offers out there, you can easily eat out several nights a week—and *never pay full price!* And you get to try out all sorts of interesting restaurants, from the familiar to novel ethnic cuisines.

Because 2-for-1 offers are intended to bring new customers into the restaurants, they are usually prominently advertised. Local newspapers are a good source. Check the dining or restaurant section of your Sunday newspaper. Or look in the weekly food section. Another great place to find 2-for-1 deals is in those free weekly newspapers you can pick up around town. These entertainment-oriented papers are chock-full of restaurant ads, with many offering specials or 2-for-1 deals. Also look through those packets of coupons from local retailers you periodically find in your mailbox.

The Red Onion, a popular chain of Mexican restaurants in Southern California, recently offered a 2-for-1 Sunday brunch special in the *Los Angeles Times.* All they asked was that the coupon in their ad be cut out and given to the waiter when you ordered. That's it. No tricks, no misleading language. Just free food for the time it takes to clip the coupon from the newspaper.

For the most complete listing of 2-for-1 offers, you may want to buy a restaurant discount book. They often list hundreds of 2-for-1 or 50 percent off deals, arranged conveniently by type of restaurant and location. These books are tops for both ease of use and sheer volume of discounts, but they're usually not free. If you are a frequent restaurant-goer, though, or would like to be, they can represent a terrific bargain: literally hundreds of free meals at your fingertips.

Perhaps the best known of these discount coupon books is the Entertainment series. ENTERTAINMENT PUBLICATIONS has discount directories covering 111 major metropolitan areas worldwide, with over 80 directories for the United States alone. The books are put out annually, and the restaurants included agree to honor their discounts for a full year. A recent local edition listed 2-for-1 discounts at 190 nearby restaurants, including everything from coffee shops to "special occasion" spots, plus 96 more discounts for fast-food, donuts, frozen yogurt, and more. Each discount may only be used once, but the tremendous variety and number of offers make this a useful book anyway.

Our local book features discounts at several restaurants that I already know and love—worth $16 at my favorite Italian place, $17 at the best Chinese restaurant in town, and $20 at a fancy restaurant that I would never be able to visit at full price. There are also discounts for movies, car washes, and all sorts of other things that make the book worth buying even if you don't eat out that often. Entertainment books are often sold through credit card companies (such as J.C. Penney's store charge card) or as fund-raisers for nonprofit organizations. For more information, contact ENTERTAINMENT PUBLICATIONS, INC., 2125 Butterfield Road, Troy, Michigan 48084, (313) 637-8400. Entertainment guides currently cost around $35.

Another well-known discount restaurant directory is PREMIER DINING CLUB, Membership Inquiries, 831 Greencrest Drive,

Westerville, Ohio 43081, (800) DINE 241. Premier Dining Club works similarly to Entertainment's offers. You order two adult entrees at one of the Club's restaurants. At the end of the meal, you present your membership card, and the restaurant's specified discount (a dollar amount or the price of the less expensive entree) is deducted from your bill.

One of the benefits of Premier is their Restaurant Locator Service. Call their toll-free number from anywhere in the United States and one of their representatives will refer you to participating restaurants from their more than 3,000 nationwide, featuring whatever type of cuisine you like. Many of Premier Dining Club's restaurants will also 2-for-1 savings on repeat visits—something Entertainment doesn't offer. The Club's Premier Savings Pack also offers discounts on hotels, car rentals, gifts by phone, and tickets to movies and other attractions. Priced at around $49, local directories are available for most major metropolitan areas.

Discount books can be a wise investment if you like to dine out a lot, but shop around. Not only do prices vary substantially, but so do services. If you are looking mainly for local restaurants, or for fast-food discounts, the Entertainment book is a good bet. Frequent travelers may find Premier Dining Club's no-extra-charge national coverage more beneficial.

The key is not to purchase one of these guides before considering how well it will serve you. If possible, look through it first. Check to see that it offers discounts at the kinds of restaurants you like to visit, and that the restaurants are located nearby. Make sure there aren't excessive restrictions on the offers, or ones that might make them difficult to use, such as discounts that are good only on weekdays, when you mainly eat out on weekends.

But if the restrictions seem reasonable, and you are happy with the variety of restaurants featured, try it—you'll have plenty of free meals to look forward to!

Other Deals for Free Meals

Don't forget about treating yourself on your birthday, either. If you're not too shy to identify yourself as a birthday boy or girl, you may get a free hunk of cake, complete with birthday candles and serenade. DENNY'S restaurants and many others will even pay for your meal, if you can show proof of your birthdate. You may not be thrilled about turning another year older, but it may be easier to accept when you know it'll earn you free food.

If you are 55 or older, look for senior citizen's specials, too. Many restaurants devote a portion of their menus to lower priced meals that are available only to seniors, and often at sizable savings. Others, such as restaurants in HOLIDAY INNS, RED LION INNS, and THUNDERBIRD MOTOR INNS, will take a specified percentage off your bill if you can prove your age or show a membership card for a senior club or organization. BOB'S BIG BOY, ROY ROGERS, and RAX RESTAURANTS, for instance, have "Senior Savings Card" programs, which entitles customers over 55 to a 10 percent discount off their parties' total bills, no matter how old their companions are. THE INTERNATIONAL HOUSE OF PANCAKES recently featured a senior special homestyle dinner for $3.99 after 4 P.M. Denny's Senior Menu has over 20 breakfast, lunch, and dinner choices, and a different dinner special every day. They reduce the portions as well as the cholesterol and salt contents of these special meals, since many of today's older adults are health and weight conscious and prefer eating smaller meals.

If you are planning a weekend away or a longer vacation, check with a travel agent about coupons for free meals, drinks, admission to shows, or even ski-lift tickets. Many hotels, chambers of commerce, and visitors' bureaus offer these coupon booklets to those who know to ask. You'll find coupons for all sorts of things that can make your vacation much more enjoyable, and save you money, too.

As always, your best bet for saving money at restaurants is to ask up front what discounts they offer. If there are none, you haven't lost anything. But if there are, you may have earned yourself a free meal!

CHAPTER 3

FREEBIES AND DISCOUNTS ON HEALTH AND BEAUTY PRODUCTS AND SERVICES

VANITY CAN BE CHEAP

Anyone who has visited a department store makeup counter lately will vouch for the fact that beauty is an expensive proposition. Prices have become so high at beauty salons and cosmetics departments that they should probably keep a supply of smelling salts on hand to revive customers suffering from sticker shock.

American women spend $30 billion at the beauty salon every year. The typical American woman visits a salon an average of 11 times a year, spending about $238 annually on salon services alone. Another $4 billion goes towards makeup. Although prices may be relatively reasonable in some salons, they can vary considerably. Manicures, for instance, can range from $5 to $22. Haircuts can cost up to $100—or more—at some salons.

Many of us are so intimidated by these high prices that we assume they must be fair. You get what you pay for, we may rationalize. Salon owners count on this attitude to keep their coffers full. As the owner of a trendy Los Angeles salon explained, his business weathers a recession better than most. "You can skip eating out in a restaurant and cook your own food at home, but you can't do your own hair," he says.

You may not want to do your own hair, but you can find terrific savings on personal grooming, without having to sacrifice anything.

Cutting the Cost of Hair

Discount family hair cutting chains are springing up all over the country. They offer basic, no-frills services—mainly haircuts—at no-frills prices.

As many of these centers are independently owned, prices may vary slightly by location, but expect to pay $9 to $10 for a cut. Shampooing and blowdrying may cost you extra, however, many places will allow you to use their equipment to style your own hair after your cut at no extra charge. It's a good idea to ask exactly what is included for your money before the stylist starts cutting. And don't assume you'll be able to set an appointment; services are normally provided on a first-come, first-served basis.

Here are a few of the biggest discount hair cutting operations:

COST CUTTERS FAMILY HAIR CARE SHOPS. (612) 331-8500. Close to 400 locations.

FANTASTIC SAM'S. (901) 363-86224. Over 1,200 locations nationwide.

GREAT CLIPS, INC. (800) 999-5959. Over 200 locations.

SUPERCUTS. (800) 999-2887. More than 500 locations nationwide.

Check for a location nearest you in the white pages of your telephone directory.

Cosmetology schools are another great way to save money on haircuts. You are pampered by advanced cosmetology students who have spent hundreds of hours working on mannequins and each other before being allowed to work on you. The students are closely supervised by expert instructors throughout, so you know your hair is safe. Expect to save 60 percent off what you'd pay in a salon for the same services: cuts, coloring, and permanents. Often these services are offered to the public one evening per week, or only between certain hours. Check your local telephone book for a cosmetology school near you, and give them a call.

Excellent low-cost hair services are also available at many full-service, full-price salons. Free and almost-free haircuts and coloring are done by licensed trainees, under the supervision of trusted professionals at locations across the country. The prices are hard to beat, but be prepared to make some sacrifices. You may have an audience during your haircut, and services may take more time than usual. But you will also be treated to the most chic, up-to-date cut you can get, and for a fraction of what you'd pay anywhere else.

Here are a few of the best deals:

- VIDAL SASSOON: Training nights are Tuesday and Wednesday. Cuts are $10, and students get an additional 20 to 30 percent discount. Locations in Chicago, Los Angeles, New York, and San Francisco. Call (212) 535-9200 for more information.

- BUMBLE AND BUMBLE: Appointments with licensed assistants available during the weekly supervised class or regular working hours. Cuts are around $5. Located in Manhattan at 146 East 56th Street. Call (212) 371-4100 for the specifics.

- CARLTON HAIR INTERNATIONAL: Free haircuts, color, and perms. Wednesdays at 7 and 9 P.M. Citywide locations in Los Ageles. (213) 475-3264.

- CHARLES IFERGAN SALON: Tuesday nights, all services are free. Cuts and color limited to techniques taught that night. Three locations in the Chicago area. Call (312) 642-4484 for details.

- JINGLES ADVANCED HAIR TRAINING CENTER: $5 cuts are given by practicing hairdressers who are learning the latest styles at this training branch of a fashionable and well-known London salon. Appointments available during regular business hours. Located at 350 Fifth Avenue in Manhattan. Call (212) 695-9365.

- NUBEST & COMPANY: Bargain night is Tuesday, when trainee cuts are $5. Located in Manhasset, NY Call (516) 627-9444 for information.
- BOGART SALON: Tuesday nights, cuts are free, color almost free. Located in Washington, D.C. Call (202) 333-6550.
- YOSH FOR HAIR: Free cuts, color, and perms on training days at their salon in Palo Alto, California. Call for details at (415) 328-4067.
- GLEMBY'S SUPER SAVER SALONS: Prices start at $7 every day. Over 1,000 salons nationwide. Call (800) 777-4444 for the specifics.
- CLAIROL EVALUATION SALON: If your hair color and type interest them, they may color your hair for free. Located at 345 Park Avenue in Manhattan, you must apply in person, Monday through Thursday. For information, call (212) 546-2713 or (212) 546-2715.
- CARLTON HAIR INTERNATIONAL: Free haircuts, color and perms. Wednesdays at 7 and 9 P.M. Citywide locations in Los Angeles. (213) 475-3264.
- SEBASTIAN INTERNATIONAL HEADQUARTERS, RESEARCH AND DEVELOPMENT LAB: Free cuts, color, and perms, 8 A.M. to 4:30 P.M. weekdays. Located in Woodland Hills, CA (818) 999-6112.

Free (and Almost Free) Cosmetics

Believe it or not, those overpriced cosmetic counters in department stores are a good source of free makeup, skin care products, and fragrances. The same places that charge $35 for

Chapter 3

foundation often give away generous samples of that same foundation for nothing. Visit your nearest department store, skin care or beauty salon, and simply ask for samples. Explain that you need to try out any cosmetics before you buy them. You will walk out with at least a handful, and maybe even more. And check the fine print in magazine ads. Often companies will send you free samples of cologne or moisturizer if you drop them a note or call a toll-free number.

Also keep your eyes open for "gift with purchase" offers. To get customers to try more of their products, most high-end cosmetics companies advertise these deals regularly. Make a minimum purchase from their line, and you receive a collection of other products to try. The free cosmetics, skin care products, and perfumes you receive are the same ones you'd pay an arm and a leg for normally.

For example:

- Princess Marcella Borghese recently offered, for an $18.50 minimum purchase, "Skin Necessities": a tube of eye treatment cream, a bottle of foundation, and a full-size lipstick that normally sells for $16 all by itself.
- Clinique frequently has "gift with purchase" offers. A recent one included clarifying lotion, moisturizer, eye cream, mascara, lipstick, and a lip brush—all for free with a $12 purchase.
- Purchase two items from Christian Dior's Monochrome collection and they throw in a full-size tube of exfoliating gel.
- For an Elizabeth Arden purchase of $12.50 or more, they recently offered a gift collection called "State of the Art," which included their Ceramide Time Complex Capsules, moisturizing sun block, cream makeup, lipstick, and a .38-ounce bottle of Red Door eau de toilette.

Cosmetics companies make these offers so regularly that it would be silly to buy their products, which are relatively expensive by themselves, while no "gift with purchase" deals are offered. Instead, look through your Sunday newspaper's magazine and lifestyle sections each week. When you see an offer from your favorite cosmetics or fragrance line, take advantage of it. Not only will you save a small fortune, you'll get to try new scents, new colors, and new products—for free.

Discounts by Mail

If you are patient, you can save a substantial amount of money by ordering cosmetics and fragrances from mail-order catalogs at excellent discounts. There are a number of catalogs that sell discontinued products, colors, and sample sizes of first-quality items at a fraction of their original cost.

BEAUTIFUL VISIONS, 810 South Hicksville Road, C.S. 4001, Hicksville, NY 11855-4001, offers products from such famous makers as Giorgio, Revlon, Max Factor, and L'Oréal at up to 90 percent off. A recent catalog featured Revlon nail enamel, regularly $3.50, for $1.49. L'Oréal lipstick was $1.99, or 62 percent off its normal $5.25 price tag.

Similar savings are available from BEAUTY BUY BOOK, G.R.I. Corporation, 65 East Southwater Street, Chicago, IL 60601. They offer prices up to 80 percent off retail on such names as Germaine Monteil, Elizabeth Arden, and Coty.

AMERICAN BOUTIQUE, Box 1756, Peoria, IL 61656, advertises discounts up to 75 percent. They carry items from Clinique, Frances Denney, Max Factor, and Charles of the Ritz, among many others.

Discounts on national brand cosmetics and fragrances are also offered by ICF, Box 76, Scarsdale, NY 10583. They'll send you a free list of their inventory.

Chapter 3

Why Pay Extra for the Name?

According to *Consumer Reports* magazine, cosmetics formulas are basically the same from one brand to another. The key differences between a high-priced lipstick and a drugstore version are packaging, fragrance, and image. These differences can raise the price considerably.

As consumers are becoming more aware of this fact, some companies are responding. Almost as soon as a new designer fragrance comes out, copycat versions appear on drugstore counters nationwide, with prices at a fraction of the original. Even experts can't usually tell the copies from the real thing.

Before you lay out a large sum of money for a name brand, see if your local drugstore offers a generic version. There are also generic versions of several brands of expensive hair care products (shampoo, conditioner, etc.). The products are almost identical in ingredients, scent, and even packaging. The only apparent difference is the price.

If you can't find copycat perfumes at a nearby store, several mail-order companies can help. ESSENTIAL PRODUCTS COMPANY, INC., 90 Water Street, New York, NY 10005, offers almost 100 years of experience in duplicating scents. Their own versions of famous men's and women's fragrances cost a small fraction of the prices of the originals.

Judged closest to the original in four out of nine cases in a study by *Shop* magazine, CLASSIQUE'S generic fragrances are among the best. Send for their price list, which features perfumes, colognes, bath oils, and face creams, by writing to Classique Perfumes, 10-02 44th Drive, Long Island City, NY 11101.

Over 200 generic versions of popular scents are available from RENAISSANCE PERFUMES, 145 South Livernois, Suite 258, Rochester, NY 48063.

TULI-LATUS PERFUMES, P.O. Box 422, Whitestone, NY 11357, makes what they call "exquisite renditions" of famous fragrances. Popular copies include their versions of Joy by Patou, Giorgio, and Calvin Klein's Obsession.

RICHELLE PARFUMES, LTD., 603 Bedford Avenue, Brooklyn, NY 11211, also sells copies of name brand fragrances, and advertises prices at up to 80 percent off the originals'.

With all of these options, you can save hundreds of dollars a year on your hair, skin, and cosmetics. You don't have to sacrifice beauty for economy.

STAY HEALTHY FOR LESS

As long as our society considers medical care a private issue and the responsibility of individual citizens, each and every one of us must assume the burden of our family's medical costs. Medical insurance premiums continue to skyrocket, with no relief in sight. Medicare and Social Security benefits are inadequate, and the costs for Medigap policies are beyond the means of many seniors.

A self-employed individual, without the benefit of medical coverage through work or a group, must spend literally thousands of dollars to protect the health of his family. As a result millions of Americans today are not able to afford the luxury of major medical or hospitalization insurance, and are living in fear of an illness or accident befalling them or members of their family.

However, the future is not as bleak as it looks. Thanks to public and private organizations, citizens groups, manufacturers, medical facilities, research groups, health associations, seniors groups, health departments of colleges and universities, etc., there *are* ways to receive high-quality free and low-cost medical care, examinations, advice, and educational information. There are also several alternatives to saving on everyday medical and preventative health care costs such as vitamins and drugs. In fact, we will show you how you can save up to 50 percent and more on these expensive, overpriced products.

In the following pages we examine various organizations, associations, and companies that provide free and low-cost medical information, services, and advice. We will give you the sources needed to ensure the continuing health of your family. Preventive health care and maintenance is available and affordable if you know where to look for it.

Everything You Ever Wanted to Know About Your Health—for Free

For residents living in the New York City area, there is a free telephone health library for the public offering tapes by Lenox Hill Hospital physicians. Audio tapes provide three to five minutes of basic information that helps callers recognize early signs of disease. The service, called TEL-MED, provides neither diagnosis nor individual medical attention.

Tel-Med offers over 200 tapes covering specific areas within a topic. Topics include:

> Alcoholism, Cancer, Seven Paths to Cancer Prevention, Human Sexuality, Kidney Ailments, Mental Health, Muscles and Joints, Nervous System Disorders, Pests and Insects, Children, Common Problems, Dental Health, Diabetes, Dieting and Nutrition, Digestive Disease, Drug Abuse, Eye, Ear, Nose, and Throat, Family Planning, First Aid, Heart and Circulatory Disease, Respiratory Disease and Allergies, Skin, Sleep Information, Public Information, Smoking, Stress and How to Cope, Sexually Transmitted Diseases, Women

To reach Tel-Med or receive a brochure explaining the service in more detail, contact: Tel-Med, Lenox Hills Hospital, Health Education Center, 1080 Lexington Ave., New York, NY 10021. (212) 439-3200. Telephone calls are accepted from 9:30 A.M. to 4:30 P.M., EST, Monday - Friday.

One of our favorite booklets, *The Consumer Information Catalog*, always features interesting free (or minimal cost) pamphlets on different aspects of health and medical care. Recent topics included: "Fitness Fundamentals," "How to Take Weight Off Without Getting Ripped Off," "Who Donates Better Blood for You Than You?" "Anabolic Steroids: Losing at Winning," "A Doctor's Advice on Self-Care," "Myths and Facts of Generic Drugs," "Food and Drug Interactions," "AIDS," "Clearing the Air: A Guide to Quitting Smoking," "The Colon," "Facing Surgery? Why Not Get a Second Opinion?," and "Do-It-Yourself Medical Testing."

To receive a free copy of this quarterly handbook, which lists over 200 useful sources of information, write: Consumer Information Catalog, Consumer Information Center, P.O. Box 100, Pueblo, CO 81002.

The Consumer Resource Handbook, free from the Consumer Information Center-N, P.O. Box 100, Pueblo, CO 81009, lists many organizations and their toll-free telephone numbers. Some examples include:

Alcohol Hotline	(800) 252-6465
Alzheimer's and Related Diseases Association	(800) 621-0379 or (800) 572-0379 in Illinois
American Cancer Society	(800)4-CANCER(422-6237)
American Council of the Blind	(800) 424-8666
American Diabetes Association	(800) 232-3472
Better Hearing Institute	(800) 424-8576
Cancer Information Services	(800) 638-6694
National Health Information Clearinghouse	(800) 336-4797
National Society to Prevent Blindness	(800) 221-3004
Parkinson's Education Program	(800) 344-7872

THE DEPARTMENT OF HEALTH AND HUMAN SERVICES, Food and Drug Administration, publishes the *FDA Consumer*, a magazine containing the latest information and findings on diet and nutrition, including reports on new medicines, their benefits and side effects. It also covers topics like sodium, osteoporosis, generic drugs, and children's vaccinations, with health advice of special concern to women. A subscription is $12 per year for 10 issues. To subscribe write: Superintendent of Documents, Washington, D.C. 20402-9371.

Free Health Care

Many health facilities, including hospitals, nursing homes, clinics, etc., give free or low-cost health care to qualified people who cannot afford to pay. Under a law passed by Congress in 1964, known as the Hill-Burton program, these facilities must provide services without discrimination on the basis of race, color, national origin, or creed. If you qualify for assistance under the guidelines published by the Department of Health and Human Services, you may receive free treatment and services. For additional information, write your Department of Health and Human Services regional office or call the toll-free hotline: (800) 638-0742 (in Maryland (800) 492-0359).

Have Your Company Pay to Keep You Healthy

Since the early 1970s, work-site health promotion efforts have grown significantly. Over two-thirds of companies across the nation with 50 or more employees have offered at least one health-promotion activity a year. Traditionally, these activities have focused on prevention of cardiovascular disease, cancer, cirrhosis, and other lifestyle-related diseases. Programs include screenings for a wide variety of disorders administered in tandem with hospitals and community agencies. Other programs including fitness and exercise, nutrition, weight control, cessation of smoking, stress management and hypertension control, have proved very successful in achieving company goals of reducing employee/retiree health care costs, improve productivity, reduce absenteeism, and improve morale.

Free and Low-Cost Health Programs in Your Community

Community medical centers and hospitals offer periodic free and low-cost health screenings. Medical screenings are also offered by private clinics that promote their services along with free tests. Look for advertisements in your local daily and weekly community newspapers announcing dates and times or call your area hospital. If you choose to attend a clinic through a private office, get the free screening or exam, then go home to "think about" any suggestions they have regarding treatment. Or make an appointment to come back at a later time. You might want to get a second opinion before incurring any additional expenses.

These screenings are often available during certain months of the year when a national organization promotes awareness and prevention of a specific disease or condition, such as "Breast Cancer Month" or "National Heart Month" or "Flu Prevention Month."

In addition to these times, there are free clinics throughout the year for blood pressure checks, cholesterol checks, cataract and glaucoma screenings. There are also free vision tests, hearing exams, foot exams, skin cancer exams, low-cost mammograms and pap smears, and flu and pneumonia vaccines. Check the calendar listing in your local newspaper for announcements of times and dates.

Seniors, Dial Help for Free

Many older people and their caregivers have trouble finding the right information in times of need. However, now there is the SENIOR HELPLINE, developed by the Gerontology Resource

Center at Brigham Young University. By calling a toll-free number, seniors living in all 50 states and Puerto Rico can hear short messages on dozens of topics.

There are four advantages to this useful service: First, messages are available 24 hours a day, 7 days a week. Second, the topics are carefully selected and tailored to meet the needs of older adults and caregivers. Third, seniors with visual or hearing impairments can gain access to useful information since the directory is available in Braille and printed copies of messages are mailed on request. Finally, those calling the Helpline are insured of complete privacy allowing them to listen as often as they like without any embarrassment.

To call the Senior Helpline, dial (800) 328-7576. For a Helpline Directory write: BYU Senior Helpline, F 274 HFAC, Brigham Young University, Provo, UT 84602.

"Health Resources for Older Women"

This is an informative and easy-to-read guide for older women that is packed with information about the normal changes that take place during the aging process as well as conditions such as arthritis and osteoporosis. The guide includes sections on menopause, nutrition and exercise, skin care and diseases, use of medicines, accident prevention, osteoporosis, osteoarthritis, housing options, nursing homes, financial planning, caregiving and widowhood. The 75-page booklet (NIA 87-2899) is available free from the U.S. Public Health Service, U.S. Department of Health and Human Services, NIA Distribution Center, 2209 Distribution Circle, Silver Springs, MD 20910.

More Special Benefits for Folks over 50

Many community hospitals have departments created specifically for the study and treatment of medical conditions that occur more frequently in mature and older adults. Known as Centers for Geriatric Health, Senior Health and Peer Counseling Centers, Senior Health Connection, etc., these departments offer free services, such as yearly vaccines and screenings. Some operate on a membership fee basis entitling those who join to additional free and low-cost health education and screening programs throughout the year. They also offer members discounts on prescription drugs and vitamins, eyeglasses, and dentistry. Many have psychiatric counseling and programs on financial planning, legal issues, Medicare, HMOs and other medical insurance alternatives. Check with your area community medical center or hospital about their services for older adults.

Quality dental care is also available for older persons regardless of their financial status. Most of the 57 dental schools in this country provide free or low-cost patient care through their clinics. Several national organizations are also involved with improving oral health among mature adults, including the American Association of Dental Schools, the American Dental Hygienists' Association, and the American Society for Geriatric Dentistry. For a list of dental schools contact the AMERICAN DENTAL ASSOCIATION, Commission on Dental Accreditation, 211 East Chicago Avenue, Chicago, IL 60611. Also check the phone book for your local Dental Society for information.

You Don't Have to Bite Off More Than You Can Chew

Many problems with teeth, gums, and other areas of the mouth are preventable. Regular check-ups can help prevent unnecessary pain, financial expenses, tooth loss, and can improve your overall health. Diseases of the mouth negatively affect the entire body, just as diseases of other parts of the body often lead to medical repercussions in the mouth. Over 100 diseases can show up in the mouth.

As mentioned above, you can receive inexpensive, quality dental care, including orthodontics, through most of the dental schools in this country. Dental hygiene programs also have special services for people who cannot afford dental insurance or private dental treatment. You can realize savings up to 60 percent on examinations and follow-up treatment if you take advantage of services provided by schools, clinics, and training programs. Check with the associations listed above or your local Dental Society.

Health Fairs and Expos

These are some of the best places to learn about staying healthy. You can find representatives from medical centers, laboratories, vitamin and drug producers, and equipment manufacturers ready and eager to share information about their products, services, and benefits. These events provide an opportunity to learn about recent medical breakthroughs, the latest treatments and therapies, new drugs and medicines, diet, nutrition and cooking tips, and exercise and fitness programs.

Free health screenings are one of the most popular and valuable attractions at these events. These include vision and hearing exams, podiatric exams, diabetic and glucose tolerance tests, mammograms, oral cancer and general dental screenings, body compositions, pulmonary function tests, blood pressure, cholesterol and stroke detection tests. Some tests may be offered for a token donation, but the health screenings alone more than pay for the admission costs. When added to all the other exhibits and demonstrations, health fairs and expos are an economical way to access your present and future health goals. For mature adults, "Time of Your Life" expos are worthwhile events that focus on nutrition, medical care, and maintenance of a healthy life-style geared towards an older age group. These expos have become increasingly popular in recent years as people are living longer, healthier and more active lives through their 60s, 70s, and 80s.

Ask the Doctor for Free

Got a question about your child's health? Ask the doctors on the PEDIATRIC HEALTHLINE at the Arnold Palmer Hospital for Children and Women, in Orlando, Florida. The toll-free service is available the first Wednesday of every month, between 6 and 9 P.M. Eastern time. The number is (800) 727-9434

The BEECH-NUT NUTRITION HOTLINE has over 40 audio tapes by doctors, nurses, and dentists regarding common childhood diseases and disorders. The toll-free numbers are: (800) 523-6333 (U.S.) and (800) 492-2384 (in Pennsylvania) You can also talk to a consumer relations agent who will discuss nutritional requirements, menus, child development, pre- and post-natal care. In addition, Beech-Nut has free guides on nutrition, allergy, and other topics. Call them between 9 A.M. and 6 P.M., EST, Monday - Friday.

Save on Saving Your Eyes

If you think you may need reading glasses (for close-up vision rather than distance vision), but don't want to spend several hundred dollars at a private optometrist or opthalmologist's office for an eye exam and prescription glasses, spend some time at your local pharmacy, drug store, or department store checking out over-the-counter reading glasses. These non-prescription glasses generally cost under $15 and come in varying strengths. Basically, they are low-powered magnifying glasses. Try the lowest magnification first and see if it improves your reading and lessens any eye strain you may have been experiencing. These glasses are especially helpful for folks over 40 whose distance vision is still good, but who are having trouble reading the fine print on menus and in paperback novels.

Free Samples for When You're Under the Weather

Every doctor is inundated with free samples of the latest antibiotics, medications, ointments, etc. Most are happy to pass them on to you for treatment of minor problems or family illnesses that generally last only a short while. Not only do these free samples save you money, but by using them up, you avoid having prescription medications that have the potential for going bad or being misused around the house for an extended period of time. When your doctor fills out your prescription, ask if he or she has any samples of the medication or one that works similarly.

Sources of Free Information and Answers to Your Medical Questions

Nearly every national organization and association associated with a particular disease or health program offers free booklets, pamphlets, screenings, toll-free information numbers, and personal counseling. A major goal of these organizations (in addition to fund raising for research and treatment) is to increase public awareness of symptoms, causes, available treatment, and steps towards prevention of these illnesses. Private companies and manufacturers of medical products are also anxious to educate the public about their products and benefits.

Support groups for nearly every type of physical, mental, or behavioral problem are available through community service groups and medical centers. These groups offer help and counseling to men, women, children, young adults, seniors, widows, families, parents of adolescents, children coping with elderly parents, families of AIDS patients, cancer patients, etc. If you or someone you know is in need of this kind of help, check with your local medical, senior citizen, or community center, church, synagogue, or school. Meetings and discussion groups are often announced in the weekly calendar or events listing of local newspapers.

Health and Beauty

The following is a list of free offers, information, and referral services covering a wide array of health-related issues:

- U.S. Department of Health and Human Services, Alcohol, Drug Abuse and Mental Health Administration, 5600 Fishers Ln., Rockville, MD 20857. Free booklets series on *Plain Talk About*... For example, *Plain Talk About Mutual Help Groups*, explains how support groups work and who can benefit from them. Also included are addresses of organizations for people with various problems.

- ANHEUSER-BUSCH, INC., (800) 359-8255 has a free two-book parents' guide offering communication guidelines, parent strategies for different age groups of children, and sample dialogues. Entitled *How to Talk to Your Kids About Drinking: A Parents Guide* and *How to Talk to Your Kids About Drinking and Driving*, the set is available by calling the above toll-free number.

- Need some help in explaining the "facts of life" to your kids? PERSONAL PRODUCTS will send you free booklets on going through puberty. Ask for them by title: *How Shall I Tell My Daughter; For Boys: A Book About Girls;* and *Growing Up and Liking It* (for girls). Write: Personal Products, Consumer Information Center, Milltown, NJ 08850.

- For a free pocket-sized First Aid guide, health record, calendar, and rescue breathing card write: INTERNATIONAL BROTHERHOOD OF ELECTRICAL WORKERS, 1125 15th St. N.W., Washington, D.C. 20005.

- JOHNSON & JOHNSON'S CONSUMER EDUCATION DEPT., New Brunswick, NJ, 08903 will send you a free "First Aid Facts" chart.

- Every family should have a booklet on household materials that are poisonous. *Save Your Child From Poisoning* is free from R.W.A.C., 151 Farmington Ave., Hartford, CT 06156.

- Cancer affects approximately 8,500 children each year. Many of these are curable with early detection, treatment and follow-up care. *The Fight Against Childhood Cancer*, a free booklet about the three most common childhood cancers, including treatment, symptoms, side effects, and recovery rates is available by sending a SASE to: St. Jude Children's Research Hospital, P.O. Box 3704, Memphis, TN 38103.

- For a free booklet on how to get your child to sleep through the night, plus ways to cope with nightmares, bed-wetting, and other sleep problems write for: *Parent/Child Sleep Guide*, Dept. P/C, Box 13, Washington, D.C. 20044.

- The American Dental Association will provide you with free information on caring for your child's teeth. Write for *Your Child's Teeth,* American Dental Association, Dept. of Public Information and Education, 211 E. Chicago Ave., Chicago, IL 60611. Ask for a list of their other free publications.

- THE TOBACCO INSTITUTE will send you a free copy of *Tobacco: Helping Youth Say No*, the third booklet in a series designed to keep parents and children communicating about important issues like smoking. Ask for copies of their other booklets as well. Write The Tobacco Institute, P.O. Box 41130, Washington, D.C. 20018.

- The *Family Guide to Vision Care* will answer questions about exams, glasses, contact lenses and eye care. Write: THE AMERICAN OPTOMETRIC ASSOCIATION, 243 No. Lindberg Blvd., St. Louis, MO 63141.

- THE AMERICAN ACADEMY OF OPHTHALMOLOGY and its participating physicians offer free eye care through the "National Eye Care Project." They will send you free information on care and diseases of the eyes, such as cataracts. Contact your local area agency for participating doctors in your area or write: American Academy of Opthalmology, P.O. Box 7424, San Francisco, CA 94120.

- If your ears are making their own noises as loud or louder than whatever external noises are around you (i.e., traffic, typewriters, printers, airplane engines, jackhammers in the street), you may be suffering from tinnitus, a condition that produces the experience of hearing a sound when no external source of sound is present. For a free copy of *Information About Tinnitus*, write AMERICAN TINNITUS ASSOCIATION, P.O. Box 5, Portland, OR 97207.

- For information regarding psoriasis, a condition which causes itchy, unsightly, rash-like skin, contact the NATIONAL PSORIASIS FOUNDATION, Suite 210, 6443 S.W. Beaverton Hwy., Portland, OR 97221.

- The National Cancer Institute's Breast Cancer Screening Consortium offers a free brochure on screenings. Send an SASE to P.O. Box 4333, Grand Central Station, New York, NY 10163-4333.

- THE PROSTATE CANCER EDUCATION COUNCIL has a free information booklet on this disease, which is treatable and curable if detected early. Write for *Prostate Cancer: Some Good News Men Can Live With*, Prostate Cancer Education Council, JAF Box 888, Dept. GH, New York, NY 10116.

- *Fighting Cancer: A Step-by-Step Guide to Helping Yourself Fight Cancer*, is a free 254-page guide on how to fight back once cancer strikes. For a copy call (800) 4-CANCER or write: Office of Cancer Communications, Public Inquiries Section, NATIONAL CANCER INSTITUTE, Bldg. 31, Rm. 10A24, 9000 Rockville Pike, Bethesda, MD 20892.

- An *Osteoporosis Exercise Booklet* of easy-to-do indoor exercises is available for $1.50 from PHYSICAL THERAPY

SERVICES of Washington, D.C., 1145 19th Street, N.W., Suite 714, Washington, D.C. 20036.

- You can also receive a free brochure telling you what you should know about estrogen, menopause, and osteoporosis from PREMARIN OSTEOPOROSIS INFORMATION CENTER, Box 5201, Miami, FL 33102
- The makers of The Estraderm Patch will send you a free menopause information pack. Write to CIBA, PMSI Sta., P.O. Box 13217, Bridgeport, CT 06673-3217 or call (800) 521-CIBA.
- Do you have a problem digesting dairy food? This common condition is called lactose intolerance and is caused by our bodies' producing less lactase, the enzyme that aids in the digestion of the milk sugar called lactose. The makers of Dairy Ease, a natural lactase enzyme digestive aid, will send you free information and a sample of their product by calling (800) 233-7500, ext. 118.
- The JOHNS HOPKINS HOSPITAL HEARING AND SPEECH CLINIC offers a free hearing screening test over the phone. To take the test call (301) 955-3434. The test is available 24 hours a day.
- The COUNCIL FOR BETTER HEARING AND SPEECH has a free resource book for people who suffer from hearing loss or speech problems. There are over 24 million Americans who experience these problems. Write them at 5021-B Backlick Road, Annandale, VA 22003 or call the Hearing HelpLine at (800) EAR-WELL. In addition, BELTONE ELECTRONICS, offers free hearing tests during May, Better Hearing Month. Contact a Beltone Electronics dealer near you for dates and locations.
- The NATIONAL HEARING AID SOCIETY will give you information about hearing aids. Their toll-free number is (800) 521-5247.

- Other organizations that offer free information or referral services to people with hearing loss include: SELF HELP FOR HARD OF HEARING PEOPLE (SHHH), 7800 Wisconsin Ave., Bethesda, MD 20814; THE AMERICAN SPEECH-LANGUAGE-HEARING ASSOCIATION, 10801 Rockville Pike, Rockville, MD 20852, (800) 638-8255; AMERICAN ACADEMY OF OTOLARYNGOLOGY, HEAD AND NECK SURGERY, One Prince St., Alexandria, VA 22314; and the SPEECH FOUNDATION OF AMERICA, (800) 922-9392.

- Questions about vitamins? For a free sample of ENER-B, vitamin B-12, plus a vitamin and mineral guide, send a SASE with 2 stamps to: Vitamin & Mineral Guide + ENER-B Biz Sample, NATURE'S BOUNTY/ENER-B, 90 Orville Dr., Bohemia, NY 11716.

- Call the makers of Nature Made vitamins for a free vitamin guide, (800) 933-8282.

- The AMERICAN HEART ASSOCIATION has many free reports and brochures concerning heart disease and preventive care. Check with your local branch of the AHA or write: The American Heart Association, National Center, 7320 Greenville Avenue, Dallas, TX 75231.

- If you are concerned about your cholesterol level and fat intake, write for the free booklet *Safeguard Your Heart*, which explains the latest facts in layman's terms. Send a SASE to: *Safeguard Your Heart* report, JTF Group, P.O. Box 2265, Vernon, CT 06066.

- You can write to THE ARTHRITIS FOUNDATION, Box 19000, Atlanta, GA 30326, for free booklets on arthritis, which is actually not a single disease, but a group of more than 100 different rheumatic disorders. There are also 70 chapters of The Arthritis Foundation throughout the country that offer courses and support resources designed to help arthritis patients and their families. You can get free information on the causes and prevention of arthritis and other afflictions from the AMERICAN RHEUMATISM ASSOCIATION, 17 Executive Park Drive, Suite 4809, Atlanta, GA 30329.

- Write the NATIONAL JEWISH CENTER FOR IMMUNOLOGY AND RESPIRATORY DISEASES for free information on respiratory diseases. Write them at: National Jewish Center, 1400 Jackson Street, Denver, CO 80206.
- For information about flu, write for *On Flu*, NATIONAL INSTITUTE OF ALLERGY AND INFECTIOUS DISEASES, Box AP, Bldg., 31, Room 7A32, Bethesda, MD 20892.
- Some people ignore leg pain, dismissing it as sore muscles or ordinary leg cramps. However, the HOECHST-ROUSSEL PHARMACEUTICAL COMPANY, suggests that you may have symptoms of P.A.D., peripheral arterial disease, which is caused by restricted blood flow to the legs because of blockage in the arteries. They will send you a free booklet entitled *Step Lively* explaining the causes of leg pain if you enclose a SASE to: CMC-MO, Dept. PAD, P.O. Box 830, Andover, NJ 07821.
- For additional information on pain related to walking, write to the CENTER FOR VASCULAR DISEASE, George Washington Medical University Center, 2150 Pennsylvania Ave., N.W., Washington, D.C. 20037 or the AMERICAN DIABETES ASSOCIATION, INC. National Center, 1660 Duke St., Alexandria, VA 22314.

THE AMERICAN ASSOCIATION FOR RETIRED PERSONS (AARP) publishes a number of useful and practical booklets and brochures containing information about a variety of health problems and conditions, many of which affect people of all ages, not just mature adults. For a complete list of their free publications write: AARP Fulfillment, 1909 K Street N.W., Washington, D.C. 20049.

Most public libraries carry a copy of the *Encyclopedia of Associations* in their reference section. Look under "Health and Medical Organizations" to contact the organization(s) dedicated to the research and study of diseases or health conditions for which you have an interest. Write for a list of their publications and resources for the public.

The NATIONAL HEALTH INFORMATION CLEARINGHOUSE, (800) 336-4797 will forward your questions to the government agency, support group, professional society or other organization that can best answer them. They also offer free publications on nutrition and health. Call between 8:30 A.M. - 5 P.M., EST, Monday - Friday.

More Sources of Helpful Information:

AIDS Hotline
(800) 342-AIDS

HIVS Hotline
(800) HIV-INFO

HEALTH AND HUMAN SERVICES DEPARTMENT
U.S. Office of Consumer Affairs
1725 I Street, NW
Washington, D.C. 20201

CENTERS FOR DISEASE CONTROL
 PUBLIC HEALTH SERVICE
U.S. Public Health Service
1600 Clifton Road, NE
Atlanta, GA 30333
(404) 639-3534

VITAMIN INFORMATION BUREAU
664 North Michigan Ave.
Chicago, IL 60611
(312) 751-2223

SECOND SURGICAL OPINION PROGRAM
Health and Human Services Dept.
Hubert Humphrey Building Room 313H
Washington, DC 20201
(800) 492-6603 (in Maryland)
(800) 638-6833 (U.S.)

AMERICAN DIABETES ASSOCIATION
(800) 232-3472
(703) 549-1500

VISION FOUNDATION
2818 Mt. Auborn Street
Watertown, MA 02172

NATIONAL DIGESTIVE DISEASES EDUCATION AND
 INFORMATION CLEARINGHOUSE
Box NDDIC
Bethesda, MD 20892

NATIONAL KIDNEY FOUNDATION
2 Park Avenue
New York, NY 10003
(212) 889-2210

NATIONAL OSTEOPOROSIS FOUNDATION
1625 Eye Street, NW
Washington, D.C. 20006
(202) 223-2226

Prescription Drugs and Vitamins for Less

There are several ways to purchase discount prescription drugs and vitamins. One way is by joining a discount food club or warehouse buying cooperative that offers either an in-house or mail-order discount pharmacy service. PACE MEMBERSHIP WAREHOUSE is one example of a national organization offering members service through a national mail-order pharmacy, MEDI-MAIL. PACE members save up to 40 percent off name-brand and generic medications.

Individuals can also take advantage of mail-order discounts. If you are on a regular schedule of maintenance drugs (i.e., for allergies, birth control, high blood pressure, arthritis, diabetes, etc.) you can benefit from using a mail-order pharmacy. These firms use registered, licensed pharmacists who fill thousands of prescriptions for organizations (such as PACE) and individuals. Two examples are:

AMERICA'S PHARMACY, P.O. Box 10490, Des Moines, IA 50306. Tel: (515) 287-6872. They advertise up to 60 percent off medicine, and more with generic medication, and 70 percent off vitamin and health care products. You send in an original doctor's prescription and choose from an extensive catalog of drugs and health care products. They will also refill prescriptions by phone once you are an established customer. Write for a free catalog or call for price quotes.

PRESCRIPTION DELIVERY SYSTEMS, 136 South York Road, Hatboro, PA 19040; (800) 441-8976. This mail-order firm sells generic nonprescription drugs, health aids, vitamins, prescription medicines for arthritis and epilepsy. Write for a free brochure.

If you are one of the 30 million members of the American Association of Retired Persons (AARP) you can benefit through its mail-order pharmacy program, which offers wholesale prices on prescription drugs, over-the-counter drugs, and medical supplies. For information on joining, write AARP Membership Division, 1909 K Street, N.W., Washington, D.C. 20049. Several other senior organizations and associations offer prescription drug services along with their other benefits.

Many health insurance plans and health cooperatives offer discount drugs, also contracted through large mail-order pharmacies. All you need is your original doctor's prescription.

If you are a mature adult you can receive special discounts off regular prescription drug prices. LUCKY STORES, operating over 100 pharmacies in California and southern Nevada, have a "Lucky 60 Club," entitling members over 60 to a 10 percent discount. CVS PHARMACIES, a chain of over 800 stores in 15 states in the Northeast and California also offer folks 60 and over, 10 percent off prescription drug prices.

As our search for the perfect combination of nutritional supplements and health maintaining/building vitamins continues, so does the growth of companies manufacturing these products. Organic vitamins, health supplements, natural foods, natural cosmetics, dietary and mineral supplements, organic household remedies—these kinds of products are carried by more than three dozen specialty mail-order catalogs, many which claim to offer quality, name-brand products at deep discounts.

Prices vary greatly among these types of products, so always compare before buying. Your local natural foods store, drug store, or market might have equally good prices on special purchases and sale items. We found our local Kmart had excellent sale prices on Nature Made brand vitamins and nutritional supplements. If you wish to receive free copies of catalogs, check the classified advertisements in health and fitness, homemaking, and food magazines.

A Word on Generic Drugs

Generic drugs are drugs on which brand-name patents have expired, allowing all manufacturers to make them. The generic counterparts are labeled by their active ingredient rather than by a name, and on an average, cost approximately 25 percent less than the leading name brand. For example, 100 Valium tablets selling for $24.55 might sell for $14.95 as the generic equivalent, diazepam. In their generic or store-brand forms over-the-counter medications, from headache relief remedies, contact lens solutions to cough medicines can save consumers up to 70 percent.

In comparing name-brand with generics, the Food and Drug Administration maintains that there is usually less than 3.5 percent variation between the two—the same amount of variation found between two batches of the same brand-name drug.

CHAPTER 4

FREEBIES AND SAVINGS IN THE HOME

As most of us know, we have entered what hopefully will become the decade of saving our planet. All around us are energy and environmental warnings, predictions, and proclamations of what will happen to the earth if we don't start taking care of it, beginning right now. Fortunately, there are ways we can save the earth and our environment, and also save money at the same time. In this chapter we will give you the ideas and sources of free and money-saving information to put you on the road towards conserving energy and resources, beginning in your home.

SAVE ON YOUR ENERGY BILLS

To start with, if you are considering buying appliances for a new house, remodeling, or just replacing your old ones, compare Energy Efficiency Rating (EER) labels. These labels are the result of government testing and standards of efficiency that show you the average yearly cost of running or operating a household appliance. Energy efficient products will end up paying for themselves in the long run with significant savings on utility bills.

For information on EER ratings, send $2 to the AMERICAN COUNCIL FOR AN ENERGY-EFFICIENT ECONOMY, 1001 Connecticut Avenue NW, Suite 535, Washington, D.C. 20036. They will send you the booklet, *The Most Energy-Efficient Appli-*

ances, which ranks the most efficient appliances, air conditioners and furnaces currently on the market.

The MAYTAG COMPANY provides free brochures to help educate consumers before they buy appliances. The advice and information apply to any brand product. Brochures on washers, dryers, dishwashers, electric ranges, microwave ovens, and gas ranges are available by writing: Consumer Education Department, The Maytag Company, One Dependability Square, Newton, IA 50208.

The AMERICAN GAS ASSOCIATION publishes a series of free booklets describing options and how they function on today's modern appliances. They cover dryers, water heaters, heating systems, and gas ranges. Write to: Consumer Information Committee, American Gas Association, 1515 Wilson Blvd., Arlington, VA 22209. They will also send you a guide to energy-efficient furnaces and appliances.

In addition, you can receive federal tax credits for energy conservation products that you purchase and install in your home. For more information ask for the free publication, *Energy Credits for Individuals*, available at local offices of the U.S. Internal Revenue Service.

Special income-tax credits are also given to individuals who install solar cooling or heating systems in their homes. Over the past several years, these credits have increased as our energy crisis becomes more widespread and critical. The necessity to use alternative methods of heating and cooling is now recognized by over 25 states granting income tax credits or deductions. THE NATIONAL SOLAR HEATING AND COOLING INFORMATION CENTER has a toll-free hotline numbers for questions on solar energy. Call them at: (800) 523-2929; in Pennsylvania call (800) 462-4983; in Alaska and Hawaii call (800) 233-3071.

You can also save on expensive service calls by contacting the customer service repair hotline if you have a major appliance that breaks down. Since average service call charges, without repairs, range from $28 (in Denver) to $37.50 (in Portland) up to

$109 (in Manhattan), if you can fix the "whats-a-ma-call-it" yourself, you can save quite a few dollars. The following are toll-free hotline numbers for manufacturers of major appliances:

GENERAL ELECTRIC	(800) 626-2000
MAYTAG	(800) 688-9900
WHIRLPOOL	(800) 253-1301
WHITE/WESTINGHOUSE	(800) 245-0600

If your appliances aren't among those brands listed, call your nearest service center and ask for the toll-free hotline number for customer repairs.

SAVINGS ON HEATING AND COOLING SYSTEMS IN THE HOME

Your local utility companies will generally pay you a free visit and evaluate your home from top to bottom and tell you where you can save on gas and electric bills. There are many places we may be unaware of, from basements to attics, where energy is being needlessly wasted. If you ask, they may even be able to recommend reputable contractors who will do the repairs and modifications they suggest.

In addition, many utilities give away free energy conservation devices such as water heater blankets, low-flow shower heads, portable electric heaters, and fluorescent bulbs. They also produce lots of free literature on conserving energy in the home. If you are a senior citizen or in a low-income bracket, check with your local utility companies to see if you qualify for a special discount. For example, in California, the Southern California Edison company provides a 15 percent discount on home electric usage to qualified low income customers. They will also provide fluorescent, energy conserving light bulbs. In fact, they recently celebrated giving away the 1-millionth compact fluorescent bulb since the program began in 1985. In addition to the giveaway program, the utility sells bulbs to customers for $13, which entitles them to a $5 rebate on their electric bill.

There are several types of fuel currently used to heat American homes: electricity, oil, liquefied petroleum gas, natural gas, solar heat, and wood. Heating through electricity is the most expensive. Heating by piped-in natural gas is the least expensive using conventional fuels. Although solar heating is expensive to install, the savings you realize in the long run, make it worthwhile to consider.*

The heat produced by these fuels is distributed throughout your home through various methods:

- Warm air systems using oil or natural gas for heat and electricity for fans.
- Hot water circulated by pumps to individual radiator units.
- Steam heat, usually found in older homes, rises through pipes to iron radiators.
- Fireplaces and wood-burning stoves.
- Electric heat using wall units, ceiling and floor heating coils, or individual space heaters.

The above systems and the fuels they use can be used efficiently or wastefully. You, as a homeowner, can save thousands of dollars a year by improving and properly maintaining your existing systems. The following sources of information will help you conserve energy and save. If you are planning to build or do extensive remodeling, having this information can also aid

---

*Note: Check into installing a passive solar system, it costs about the same to build as a conventional house with the advantage of 50 to 70 percent reduction on utility bills. Basic passive solar options include direct gain (using large south facing windows), solar walls, greenhouses and solar roofs.

Chapter 4

you in making decisions as to which is the best method to use in your new or newly remodeled home.

Solar Energy and Your Home, and *Learning About Renewable Energy* are free publications that answer frequently asked questions about installing solar energy and how it works. Write: CARIERS, Renewable Energy Information, Box 8900, Silver Springs, MD 20907. You can also call them about information on alternate energy sources and renewable sources, such as wind farms, alcohol fuels and solar energy. Use the toll-free numbers listed for the National Solar Energy Heating and Cooling Center.

The National Solar Energy Heating and Cooling Center also publishes free information on solar energy. Write them at P.O. Box 1607, Rockville, MD 20850.

The BORG-WARNER CORPORATION, P.O. Box 1592, York, PA 17405 will send you their free booklet, *Energy and Your Home*, describing ways to save on home heating and cooling costs.

The ALLIANCE TO SAVE ENERGY also has a free guide, *Saving Energy Booklet*, with inexpensive ways to cut down on energy costs. For a copy write: The Alliance to Save Energy, 1925 K Street, N.W., Washington, D.C. 20006.

We recommend you send for a free copy of *Your Keys to Energy Efficiency*, S. James, Consumer Information Center-N, P.O. Box 100, Pueblo, CO 81002. Also ask for a copy of the latest edition of the *Consumer Information Catalog*, which lists over 200 free and inexpensive booklets on a variety of subjects. We receive every edition of this extremely useful publication and order new booklets from it regularly. For example, our latest catalog lists, *Heating with Wood*, ($1) which includes information about buying, installing, and using wood stoves, fireplaces, furnaces, and fuel efficiently and safely.

The AVON company wants you to conserve energy safely and will send you their free pamphlet *Safe Ways to Save Energy* with information on space heaters, coal, and wood stoves, lighting, water heaters, and insulation. Their address is: Avon Products,

Inc., Consumer Information Center, 9 West 57th Street, New York, NY 10019.

RODALE PRESS, a long time leader in the field of conservation publications, has several books on energy-saving systems and alternative heating/cooling methods for the home. Write them for a copy of their current catalog: Rodale Press, 33 E. Minor Street, Emmaus, PA 18049.

THE BETTER HEATING-COOLING COUNCIL has a free booklet that explains the advantages of hot water heating and separate air conditioning systems compared to a ducted combination heating/cooling system. Send for a copy to: Practical Homeowner, Resources!, P.O. Box 5341, Pittsfield, MA 01203. Also write them for a free booklet on clean burning stoves and a free energy savings guide.

For help in selecting the right air conditioner, send $3 to the AMERICAN COUNCIL FOR AN ENERGY-EFFICIENT ECONOMY, 1001 Connecticut Ave., N.W., Suite 535, Washington, D.C. 20036. Ask for the current edition of *The Most Energy-Efficient Appliances*.

THE TECHNICAL INFORMATION CENTER, a service of the U.S. Department of Energy publishes a series of free energy saving booklets for consumers. Write them at: Technical Information Center, U.S. Dept. of Energy, Box 62, Oak Ridge, TN 37831.

Also check your local library for books on the subject of solar energy, installation, and savings.

VERMONT CASTINGS publishes a 68-page catalog on advances in woodburning technology, wood- and coal-burning stoves, fireplace systems and freestanding fireplaces. For a free copy write: *The Fireside Advisor*, Dept. IPCI, 100 Prince Street, Randolph, VT 05060.

For more free information on heating with wood send for the following:

Chapter 4

- *Turn Your Fireplace Into a Beautiful Energy Producer*, ASHLEY, P.O. Box 128, Florence, AL 35631. Ashley is a producer of glass-door fireplace heaters.
- *How Does Your Chimney Stack Up?* and *Wood-Nature's Housewarming Gift*, Wood Heating Alliance, 1101 Connecticut Ave., N.W., Washington, D.C. 20036.
- *Heatilator Planning Guide*, Heatilator Inc., 1915 W. Saunders St., Mt. Pleasant, IA 52641 (enclose a self-addressed stamped envelope).

FREE FIREWOOD FOR YOUR FIREPLACE AND WOOD-BURNING STOVE

The U.S. FOREST SERVICE, a division of the Department of Agriculture offers free downed or dead wood for firewood from any of our 155 National Forests. First you must get a permit from the forest of your choice. You are allowed up to six cords of wood (equal to about 12 loads in a pick-up truck.) With the going rate of $150 for a cord of firewood, this is worth nearly $1,000. The following are the addresses of the regional offices of the U.S. Forest Service:

NORTHERN REGION: Federal Building, 200 East Broadway St., P.O. Box 7669, Missoula, MT 59807. Tel: (406) 329-3511.

INTERMOUNTAIN REGION: Federal Building, 324 25th St., Ogden, UT 84401. Tel: (801) 625-5354.

EASTERN REGION: 310 West Wisconsin Avenue, Milwaukee, WI 53203. Tel: (414) 291-3693.

PACIFIC NORTHWEST REGION: 319 S.W. Pine St., Portland, OR 97204. Tel: (503) 221-2877.

PACIFIC SOUTHWEST REGION: 630 Sansome St., San Francisco, CA 94111. Tel: (415) 556-0122.

ROCKY MOUNTAIN REGION: 11177 West Eighth Ave., P.O. Box 25127, Lakewood, CO 80225. (303) 236-9431.

SOUTHWESTERN REGION: Federal Building, 517 Gold Ave., S.W., Albuquerque, NM 87102. Tel: (505) 842-3292.

SOUTHERN REGION: 1720 Peachtree Avenue, Atlanta, GA 30309. Tel: (404) 347-4191.

ALASKA REGION: Federal Office Building, 709 West Ninth St., Juneau, AK 99802. Tel: (907) 586-8863.

For more information write: Firewood # 559, U.S. Forest Service, Box 2417, Washington, D.C. 20013. Ask for their free booklets, *Firewood For Your Fireplace*, and *Firewood From National Forests*.

FREE CHRISTMAS TREES, WOODEN POLES, POSTS AND SEEDLINGS

Once you've gathered your free wood for keeping warm in the winter, how about some free trees to beautify the outside of your house?

The U.S. DEPARTMENT OF THE INTERIOR, BUREAU OF LAND MANAGEMENT will allow nonprofit organizations to cut trees for free. Private individuals and commercial organizations may also participate in the program for a nominal fee (usually between $3 – $5). The trees are located on federal land in 11 Western states. Once you receive a permit from the local BLM office, you are given a map with directions as to which areas are permissible for tree-cutting.

The Minor Forest Products program also allows you to collect or cut a specific number of small trees to use as poles or posts. You can also obtain free and low-cost cactus or plant seedlings from areas of natural growth where there are abundant supplies. In Southern California, local fire stations offer up to six trees per household of pine, cedar, and cypress seedlings. The free trees, in addition to being in large supply, also aid residents in maintaining a fire-safe environment.

For more information regarding these programs contact the Bureau of Land Management, Forestry Division, 18th & C Sts., N.W. Washington, D.C. 20240, (202) 653-8864, or your local BLM, U.S. Department of the Interior.

Free Trees for the Adventurous

You can also look for wild seedlings in the early spring. Search out wooded areas of your neighborhood for small seedling trees. Look for healthy, noncrowded trees. Dig them out at the rootball, replant them, lightly prune them and watch them grow into adult trees. You can also take cuttings from evergreens and place them in plastic bags, with a mixture of sand and peat moss. Thoroughly moisten, close the bags, and set them in filtered light. Keep them moist and in about two weeks you will see roots forming. Repot the cuttings in richer soil until they grow large enough for transplanting in the ground.

FREE INFORMATION ON HOME INSULATION

Rising fuel costs and the ongoing crisis in the Middle East point to the fact that, now, more than ever, properly installed, safe insulation is a major factor in saving money on heating and cooling our homes. In fact, industry experts see insulation as this country's practical hedge against rising energy costs.

Insulation is rated by *R-value*, which indicates the material's ability to Resist the flow of heat. The higher the R-value, the greater the insulating power. But how much insulation is enough? What kind of materials should you be installing in your home? What about meeting safety precautions and fire specifications?

There are several sources of information that explain the differences in insulation products, rating systems, applications, etc. For a free copy of the most recent *Certified Product Manufacturers Directory* contact NATIONAL ASSOCIATION OF HOME BUILDERS NATIONAL RESEARCH CENTER, Dept. PH, 400 Prince Georges Blvd., Upper Marlboro, MD 20772.

The FLORIDA SOLAR ENERGY CENTER, Public Information Office, Dept. PH, 300 State Road 401, Cape Canaveral, FL 32920 will send you a free information packet on radiant barriers.

The MINERAL INSULATION MANUFACTURERS ASSOCIATION has informative consumer booklets from 25 to 75 cents. They can be ordered from: Dept. PH, 1420 King St., Alexandria, VA 22314.

Most manufacturers of insulation products will send you free information on their products. Look through current issues of home-building and remodeling magazines for manufacturers' advertisements. They usually include a coupon or toll-free number for a free brochure. For example, OWENS-CORNING FIBERGLASS, Fiberglass Tower, Toledo, OH 43659, (800) 447-3759 publishes a series of pamphlets on insulation and energy saving including: *All About Insulation, Owens-Corning Fiberglass*, and a 32-page *Homeowner's Guide to Insulation and Energy Savings* that also explains new government insulation recommendations.

For a free brochure explaining what the recommended insulation levels are in your geographic region write for: *How Much Insulation Does Your Home Really Need?*, CERTAINTEED HOME INSTITUTE, P.O. Box 860, Valley Forge, PA 19482. The brochure talks about R-value and the different types of insulation materials on the market today.

WINDOWS AND WINDOW TREATMENTS CAN SAVE YOU MONEY, TOO

Insulated glass, tinted glass, decorator glass, coated glass, solar shades, reflective shades, quilted and insulated shades, vertical blinds, miniblinds, shutters, and screens. These are some of the choices you have in window and window covering products if you are building, remodeling, or decorating your home. Many offer efficient, money saving advantages over older or outdated products.

Again, most manufacturers are more than happy to send you free information explaining the beauty and energy-saving technology of their products. For example:

- FORD GLASS produces a product called transparent insulation." Call them for a free brochure at (800) GLASS-HR.

- SUNGATE PPG INDUSTRIES explains the advantages of energy-saving coated low-E glass in a free booklet called *The Intelligent Window*. Write them at: PPG Industries, Inc., Sungate Marketing Group, P.O. Box 8727, Harrisburg, PA 17105.

- ANDERSON CORPORTATION INC. Box 12, Bayport, MN 55003 will send you a free 16-page *Window and Patio Door Factbook*.

- MARVIN WINDOWS, Warroad, MN 56763, has several free pamphlets on window treatments with energy efficient features.

With so many manufacturers and products in the marketplace, we suggest using the "Reader Information Services" or "Product Information Cards" that appear in the back of decorating and building magazines for gathering information. In most cases you can check off several resources at once and then simply wait for the information to start arriving in the mail. One stamp, one card, and lots of free information.

The *Better Homes and Gardens* series of special-interest magazines contains excellent features and a wide variety of information sources for readers. Check in the back of their magazines for "Information Worth Waiting For." A recent issue of *Home Plan Ideas* offered the *Window Questions & Answers Brochure* from GREAT LAKES WINDOW, INC. This free publication answers questions about R-factors, low-E glass, fusion welding, and more. For a copy write: Home Plan Ideas, Spring 1991, Dept. HPSP1, P.O. Box 2724, Boulder, CO 80329-2724.

DON'T BE A DRIP—SAVE WATER AND SAVE $$$

Certain sections of our country are lucky. They always have water, and often much more than they can possibly use. However, in other areas, such as the Southwest, Nevada, and Southern California water is a scarce, precious commodity. Recent prolonged droughts have necessitated government implementation of mandatory water rationing. In our efforts to save money as well as save the environment, we should all pay attention to the amount of water we consume in our homes.

Some simple ways to conserve on water (and save on water and heating bills) include:

- Take shorter showers.
- Run your dishwasher only with full loads; use the energy-saving drying cycle.
- Flush your toilets less and put a container filled with water, rocks, etc., in the tank to displace water.
- Wash clothes only when you have enough for a full load.
- Always use the water-level dial on your washing machine that indicates how big a load you're putting in.

Chapter 4

- Buy a water-saving toilet or put bricks in your existing tank.
- Check for leaks around the house: dripping faucets and shower heads, running toilets, sprinklers, and hose turn-ons.
- Turn off the water while you're brushing your teeth or washing your hair.
- Whenever possible, wash dishes, clothes, and yourself with cold or warm water.
- Lower the thermostat on your water heater (for every 10 degrees you lower it, you can save nearly 10 percent on water heating energy).
- Wrap your water heater in a special insulating blanket to prevent heat loss.

To aid you in your quest to save water, write for the following:

- A free illustrated guide on finding leaks in toilets from Fluidmaster, P.O. Box 4264, 1800 Via Burton, Anaheim, CA 92803. The guide also includes a dye sample for testing for leaks and ways to correct them.
- A free water restrictor for your shower head from CON EDISON that can help an average family save thousands of gallons of water a year. Write to Con Edison, Consumer Affairs, Room 1625-S, 4 Irving Place, New York, NY 10003.
- *Water Conservation Checklist for the Home*, Superintendent of Documents, U.S. Government Printing Office, Washington, D.C. 20402 ($.70).

Also check with your local water company for free water saving kits and information.

SAVINGS IN THE GARDEN

Rodale Press, the frontrunner in environmental and conservation publications, will send you a free booklet on *How to Grow an Organic Garden in a Nutshell*, which includes a plan for a raising pesticide-free, chemical-free vegetables. Write them at: Organic Gardening & Farming, 33 E. Minor St., Emmaus, PA 18049.

Interested in starting a money-saving community garden? Write: GARDENS FOR ALL, 180 Flynn Ave., Burlington, VT 05401, for their free booklet, *Community Garden*. By working together, you and your neighbors can share and save on a variety of fruits and vegetables.

Most seed (flower and vegetable), bulb, and lawn nurseries and growers will gladly send you free catalogs, garden plans, and planting guides. Check with your local nursery for names and addresses of growers. Mail-order companies often advertise their free offers in home and garden magazines and general consumer publications.

Lawn and garden care product manufacturers are also eager to supply home gardeners with information on tending and improving their gardens. SCOTT LAWN PRODUCTS will answer questions about lawns, pests, fertilizing, watering, dead spots, etc., on their toll-free hotline, (800) 543-TURF. They will also send you a free two-year subscription to *Lawn Care* magazine and other information to help you grow and keep a healthy lawn.

ORTHO will send you a whole host of helpful books with gardening information and tips. For copies of these free books write for Ortho's Lawn & Garden Care Books, Ortho Division, Chevron Chemical Co., P.O. Box 7144, San Francisco, CA 94120.

For making your garden grow, there are lots of places to find free soil conditioners and plant food. If you want to make your own compost, save grass clippings, decomposed leaves, chopped leaves, hay, hedge trimmings, kitchen scraps, fish waste, corn husks, and wood ashes. These add good sources of nitrogen and potassium to your garden food.

Chapter 4

The EXTENSION SERVICES section of the U.S. Department of Agriculture offers free manure to gardeners. Contact the local office of the Department of Agriculture. Or check with a nearby stable, dairy, or poultry farm. The neighborhood kid down the block may even supply you with what you need from his pet rabbit.

BE SAFE AND SAVE

One area we are all concerned with these days is the security and safety of our homes. The peace of mind that comes from knowing your home and its contents are protected from fire, theft, and other intrusions is well worth the effort it may take to learn about different types of security systems. According to the FEDERAL BUREAU OF INVESTIGATION, a burglary is taking place somewhere in this country every 10 seconds. In addition, the FBI and the NATIONAL BURGLAR AND FIRE ALARM ASSOCIATION have released some alarming figures:

- More than 3 million burglaries take place each year.
- Two out of three burglaries involve private homes.
- One in 14 homes gets burglarized each year.
- Fires destroy around $6 billion in property in homes and businesses each year.
- Burglars get away with nearly $9 billion in property.

There are several excellent, free sources of information that can aid you in learning about methods of safeguarding your home. You can spend less than $50 on hardware for your doors and windows or up to $5,000 on an elaborate home-security system. Once you have done your research, you can make an informed and practical decision as to what kind of system to choose, and what steps you are going to take.

For information on alarm systems send $1 to the NATIONAL BURGLAR AND FIRE ALARM ASSOCIATION, 1133 15th St., N.W., Washington, D.C. 20005. Ask for the booklet *Considerations When Looking for a Burglar Alarm System.* STATE FARM INSURANCE will send you free advice on how to safeguard your home from fire and burglary. Write them at: State Farm Insurance, 1 State Farm, Plaza, Bloomington, IL 61701.

As in other areas of industry, manufacturers are more than willing to send interested individuals helpful information and guides about their products. They do the research and writing and you get a free education with no obligation or strings attached. For example:

- ADT SECURITY SYSTEMS, 1 World Trade Center, New York, NY 10048 will send you a free guide, *Safe at Home*, with ideas about home security and fire protection.

- *How to Protect Your Home and Family Against Burglary*, a guide to home security, is free from KWIKSET DIVISION, EMHART INDUSTRIES, 5169 Santa Ana St., Anaheim, CA 92803.

- *The Amgard Security Planning Guide*, describes your choices in home security alarm systems. Write to: AMGARD CORPORATION, 33A-2J, Ada, MI 49355.

- Learn how to better protect your home and family and also about affordable, easy to install home security systems with SCHLAGE LOCK COMPANY'S booklet, *Home Security Tips.* Call them tollfree at: (800) 562-1570.

- For those of you who would like to see the benefits of a home security system, the ALERT CENTRE PROTECTIVE SERVICES will send you a free video called "Understanding Home Security." Write them at: Prestonwood Junction, 5290 Belt Line Road, Suite 116, Dallas, TX 75240 or call (214) 991-0021.

FREE GAS-SAVING TIPS FOR YOUR CAR

In the oil-dependent world we live in, gasoline prices are about as stable as world economic conditions. And as we have seen over the past couple years, that can be pretty volatile. Although we are at the mercy of the oil companies' pricing strategies, there are ways we can individually conserve on the gas we consume and save money in the process. The MOTOR VEHICLE MANUFACTURERS ASSOCIATION has a free booklet entitled *Your Way to Better Fuel Economy*. For a copy write: Publications List, Motor Vehicle Manufacturers Association, 300 New Center Building, Detroit, MI 48202.

The AAA MOTOR CLUB has free information with gas saving tips and cost estimates for driving and owning different types of cars. Write for *Your Driving Costs* and *Gaswatchers' Guide*, AAA, 8111 Gatehouse Road, Fall Church, VA 22047.

The SHELL OIL COMPANY has produced an extensive series of pamphlets on savings for your car and home, including *The Conservation Book*, *The Home Energy-Saving Book*, *The Home Security Book*, and *The Gas Mileage Book*. Ask for them at your local Shell service station or write: Shell Answer Books, P.O. Box 61609, Houston, TX 77208.

It goes without saying that you should be pumping your gas at the "self-service" rather than "full-service" pumps. This alone will save you hundreds of dollars a year. In addition, UNOCAL service stations offer free smog checks and emission control system tuneups for pre-1975 cars. They will perform these services in a year when a smog inspection is not required by the Department of Motor Vehicles.

If you are concerned about the safety and reliability of products you plan on purchasing or those that have previously been installed in your home, contact the U.S. CONSUMER PRODUCT SAFETY COMMISSION toll-free hotline: (800) 638-8326; in

Maryland (800) 492-8363; in Alaska, Hawaii, Puerto Rico, and the Virgin Islands (800) 638-8337.

The *Consumer's Resource Handbook* (revised yearly) includes extensive listings of contacts to assist with consumer problems. It includes corporate consumer representatives, private dispute resolution programs, automobile manufacturers, and federal, state, county, and city government agencies with consumer responsibilities. It also provides information on how to avoid purchasing problems and how to write and effective complaint letter. This valuable 100-page booklet is free from the Consumer Information Center, Pueblo, CO 81009.

Last but not least, the RADIO SHACK stores, have an offer that helps solve the pesky chore of replacing batteries. It seems that we're always in need of new batteries for our flashlights, tools, remote controls, portable tape recorders, stereos, and the dozens of battery powered toys that our kids simply must have this year. You can ease the "battery battle" by joining Radio Shack's Battery-a-Month-Club. Walk into any participating Radio Shack and ask for a free "Battery Card." This entitles you to one free Radio Shack battery a month for one year. You can get cards for each member of your family and collect enough batteries for a whole year.

LIVE IN A MANSION—RENT-FREE AND FOR NO MONEY DOWN

This is one of the best-kept secrets to saving money on living expenses. You can live in beautifully furnished homes and mansions for free. There are several ways to beat the high cost of housing, but most people are unaware of these great opportunities.

One way to live rent-free is to house- and pet-sit for folks while they are on vacation or traveling. Most people would rather not abandon their precious pets to a strange kennel while they are gone. Their pets hate them for it, and most kennels have dubious reputations, at best. Also, for folks who like to keep more unusual animals, like birds, fish, turtles, horses, etc., it's not always easy to find a willing neighbor to come over and feed them, change their water, and tend to them if something goes wrong.

A professional housesitter can spend nearly all year helping different folks out by watching their houses and pets. We have several friends who own homes in other areas, or take extended trips for a month or more. They want to make sure their valuables are watched and taken care of while they are gone. In addition to pets, this includes watering plants, calling repairmen in case of emergencies, and inhabiting the premises so it doesn't appear empty to would-be burglars and intruders. The peace-of-mind in knowing that somebody is watching your home can help ensure a relaxing and worry-free vacation.

To become a house-sitter, run ads in local newspapers that circulate the more affluent neighborhoods in your area. Make sure you have good personal references for your prospective clients to call. Put notices up on bulletin boards in markets, drug stores, veterinary offices and pet stores. Pretty soon word-of-mouth recommendations should keep you 'sitting pretty' throughout the year. One house-sitter we know is booked up almost a year in advance. Her summer vacations are spent living in other people's townhouses, mansions, and estates.

Free house-sitting works in the opposite way as well. People who own expensive homes in resort and vacation areas often visit these homes only once or twice a year. When they arrive for their vacations, you can go visit friends or relatives or, as is often the case, you can move into a guest room, while they are vacationing in "your" home. How does year-round living in Key West, Florida; Kannapali Beach, Maui; Aspen, Colorado; or Malibu, California sound? Many people have homes in the Bahamas, Mexico, and other foreign countries that they prefer to be lived in year-round. A good way to offer your services and find these opportunities is to place classified ads in local newspapers, travel magazines, and metropolitan magazines, such as *Los Angeles, Arizona Living*, or *New York* magazine.

Another way to live rent-free is to house-sit for homes that are empty and for sale. Houses build for "spec" and model homes especially are perfect for house-sitting. They may not be fully furnished, but often their owners are willing to rent furniture to make the place look less empty and more "lived-in." Higher-priced homes often stay on the market for several months at a time. Meanwhile, you are living in a brand new home. Older homes up for sale are often left empty because the owners have already moved into new homes they've purchased. Fine homes with swimming pools, tennis courts and lush gardens need someone to watch over them so that vandals don't take advantage of their being empty for long periods of time.

If you have a green thumb you might want to explore the possibility of becoming a gardener or caretaker for a large estate. Rather than pay for these services, many people would rather exchange a guest house or garage apartment to a trust-worthy tenant. Most gardening and caretaking positions don't require full-time, on-the-job care, so if you are a student or want to take other jobs to supplement your income, this is a perfect opportunity.

As many of us already know, apartment and condominium managers often receive free rent in exchange for their managing and maintenance duties. Again, these duties usually require services only part-time, during the evenings or on weekends. The rest of the time is free for other pursuits.

CHAPTER 5

READ, LISTEN AND LEARN A LOT FOR LESS

FREE MAGAZINES AND NEWSLETTERS

It's becoming more common these days for magazine publishers to offer free gifts or premiums to new subscribers. We all have seen those *Sports Illustrated* advertisements that hawk free football- or sneaker-shaped phones if you buy a year's subscription to the magazine. Even venerable *Time* magazine has offered the occasional tempting premium.

A free gift is certainly a nice thing to receive when offered, be it a telephone or a tote bag. But more often than not, we can live without the subscription premiums. As least we have this far. What we would really like are the magazines. Why else would we be thinking about subscribing to them. Wouldn't it be nice to skip the "free" premium that cost you $36 for a subscription and, instead, get the magazine—what you really wanted anyway—for free?

In this chapter we will show you how to get free issues of those magazines you love to read. You can start receiving your favorite magazines and newsletters, and even some new ones, in the mail within weeks, simply by taking advantage of the publishers' own offers. This is a great way to keep current, informed, and learn more about nearly everything from investments to decorating to travel and sports.

119

Why Publishers Need You on Their Lists

Most magazines don't make their money on subscriptions or newsstand sales. They depend on advertisers, who are willing to pay large amounts of money to show off their products, to meet the expenses of a glossy, full-color magazine. The more readers a magazine can claim to have, the more potential buyers an advertiser will reach.

Getting new subscribers is much more important to a magazine than it appears at first. (We even know of a specialty investment magazine that sends some subscribers three copies of the same issue, changing the name of the addressee each time. By sending out more magazines, their subscription base appears much larger to their advertisers. When this happens, we just give the extra copies to friends who are more than happy to read them for free.)

How to Get Free Magazines

Publishers desperately want to add new names to their subscription list. If they think you want to become a subscriber once you see a sample of their magazine or newsletter, they may offer up to three months of free sample copies. Many lesser-known publications use these one-time samples to get broad, national exposure. The publishers hope that once you know they exist, you will subscribe. However, you are never under any obligation to do so. All you have to do is accept the sample copy—for free.

For example, if someone in your family is interested in star gazing, you can get a free copy of *Sky and Telescope* magazine. Write to SKY PUBLISHING CORPORATION, 49 Bay Street Road, Cambridge, MA 02138.

Those of us with more down-to-earth concerns will be interested in Mary Ellen's *Best of Helpful Hints* newsletter. It arrives packed with time- and money-saving household tips. Contact: MARY ELLEN ENTERPRISES, 6414 Cambridge Street, St. Louis Park, MN 55426, for a free sample copy.

Chapter 5

Expectant parents can receive a free subscription to *American Baby* magazine. Send your name and address and the date your baby is due to: AMERICAN BABY MAGAZINE, 352 Evelyn Street, Paramus, NJ 07652. Not only will the publishers send you the subscription, but they will also send you a free copy of *The First Year of Life*—an excellent guide on a baby's first 12 months.

PAMPERS will send you a free subscription to *Baby Care* magazine with articles chosen especially for your baby's age. Just send them your baby's birthdate and they will send the right magazine at the right time up to 9 months.

Stepfamilies will find the *Life in Step* newsletter both interesting and informative. For dealing with many of the difficulties they face everyday, including handling holidays and family get-togethers. For a free one-year subscription, enclose a self-addressed, stamped envelope and send it to: CLASSIC CHRONICLES, 7 South Lincoln, Hinsdale, IL 60521.

If you are a salesperson, or are considering switching to a career in sales, you will be interested in a free six-month subscription to *Specialty Salesman*. Write to SPECIALTY SALESMAN, Department 812-1, 307 North Michigan Ave., Chicago, IL 60601.

Salespeople and opportunity seekers will also want to send for the free five-month subscription offered by *Opportunity* magazine. Write: OPPORTUNITY, 6 North Michigan Ave., Chicago, IL 60602. As with all of these publications, they ask that you respond only if you are new to the magazine, not a current subscriber.

They may not be your typical magazine publisher, but the Soviet Embassy will be glad to send you a copy of *Soviet Life* magazine, along with other literature on Russia—for free. This is a great idea for both kids and adults who have always wanted to learn more about life in the U.S.S.R. Send your name and address to: Embassy of the U.S.S.R, 1706 18th Street Northwest, Washington, D.C. 20009.

Animal lovers will be happy to know that many animal-related magazines offer sample copies for free. *Feline and Canine Times* is a newsletter put out by FELINE AND CANINE FRIENDS, Inc., a nonprofit animal welfare group. Send a self-addressed, business-sized envelope to: Feline and Canine Friends, Inc., 505 North Bush Street, Anaheim, CA 92805, and they will send you a free copy.

Animal welfare is the subject of *Animals' Agenda*, a monthly news magazine. Articles, interviews, news, and reviews focused on the rights and welfare of animals. Write to THE ANIMALS' AGENDA, P.O. Box 5234, Westport, CT 06881 for a free sample copy.

The Los Angeles Society for the Prevention of Cruelty to Animals publishes *Time for Animals*, and will be happy to send you a free copy. Send your name and address to: Los Angeles Society for the Prevention of Cruelty to Animals, 5026 West Jefferson Blvd., Los Angeles, CA 90016. You'll also receive a collection of news, poems, book reviews, and articles.

Voice of the Voiceless is another magazine that is concerned with the welfare of animals. For a free copy of this illustrated, monthly magazine, contact VOICE OF THE VOICELESS, P.O. Box 17403, Foy Station, Los Angeles, CA 90017.

Cat lovers will find lots of up-to-date information on the welfare of cats from the NATIONAL CAT PROTECTION SOCIETY, P.O. Box 6218, Long Beach, CA 90806.

If someone you know fancies garlic in their cooking, the FRESH GARLIC ASSOCIATION will send you a free copy of their quarterly newsletter on the benefits and uses of garlic. Write to: Garlic Newsletter, P.O. Box 2410, Sausalito, CA 94966-2410.

The Jolly Green Giant will send you free newsletters with coupons, recipes, fun activities, and news from the "Valley" for joining the SPROUT'S FAMILY HEALTH CLUB. Just send your name, address and the names of your children to: Sprout's Family Health Club, P.O. Box 600163, El Paso, TX 88560.

Finally, if you stop by a PELLA WINDOW STORE (call 800-524-3700 for a location near you) to look at windows and skylights, they will give you a complimentary 1-year subscription to *Metropolitan Home, Traditional Home, Better Homes and Gardens*, or *Country Home*. Look for Pella advertisements and coupons in current issues of these magazines (offer good until 12/91).

Chapter 5

Get Your Favorite Magazines for Free, Too

Many other publications offer free sample copies. Keep your eyes open when you're reading magazines and newspapers, and when you're visiting your favorite stores. You will be surprised at what you can get—for free.

Better-known magazines, however, don't usually offer free sample copies. The publishers figure that you can always *buy* yourself a "sample" at the newsstand. But they are still concerned with fattening up their lists of subscribers.

Publishers of popular magazines assume that you've seen their publications. They hope you will like them well enough to subscribe to them. Just in case you aren't sure about committing to a one-year (or longer) subscription, they frequently offer free issues—if you let them sign you on for a period of time.

You agree to accept one or more issues of the newsletter or magazine—for free—and unless you cancel, they put you in for a regular subscription. The key to remember is that the first copy, or copies, are free. You are not obligated to continue the subscription, or to pay any money, *as long as you write "cancel" across the bill and send it back to them.* You get to keep the free issues, and your only expense is the postage stamp you'll use to return that first bill. In return, you can have a mailbox full of free magazines, simply for taking the publishers at their word.

Most of these offers will come to you as what other people call "junk" mail. Some of it undoubtedly is junk. But if you open your mailbox to find a postage-paid envelope from a magazine publisher, *don't throw it away*—it may be worth free magazines.

Our mailbox has yielded many such offers, for all types of publications, from business journals to decorating guides to fashion magazines. Here are a few examples:

- *PC/Computing, Macworld,* and *Byte* all offered free issues of their computer enthusiasts' magazines. (*Macworld* even threw in a free mouse pad with their offer).

- *Home* and *Architectural Digest* offered free decorating and remodeling magazines.
- The publishers of *Allure* will send you free samples of their fashion and beauty magazine.
- *Eating Well* and *Health Confidential* volunteered sample copies to teach us about eating and staying healthy.
- *Inc., Entrepreneur, Barron's, The Kiplinger Washington Letter*, and *Business Week* offered free business and financial publications.
- *Insight* (the excellent magazine of the *Washington Post*), *The World & I*, and *Bottom Line Personal* newsletter will keep you informed of interesting local, national, and international happenings and events for free.
- *Consumer Reports* will send a free sample issue, a free current buying guide and a free copy of *The New Medicine Show*. If you decide to subscribe you pay the subscription price; if not, you can return the invoice marked "cancel," owe nothing and keep everything they've sent.
- Both the young and the "young at heart" can enjoy a free issue of *Game Player's Strategy Guide for Nintendo Games*.
- If you're a horse lover, you can receive a free copy of *Practical Horseman* or *Performance Horseman*.
- If you are interested in exploring the by-ways to inner peace and methods to unlock the powers of your body, mind, and spirit, you can get a free copy of the *New Age Journal*.

"Serious" investment/financial magazines and newsletters are also anxious for you to try their publications. Newsletter publishers are especially interested in having you try a sample issue, hoping you will become a future subscriber and purchase their other products and services. Some examples of those offering free, no obligation sample issues include:

- *Futures and Options World*, a monthly publication from the United Kingdom focusing on international futures and options markets.
- *Consensus*, a national futures and financial weekly newspaper.
- *OTC Stock Journal*, a weekly publication featuring low-priced stock information.
- *Commodity Closeup*, a commodity newsletter and telephone hotline. Receive a one-month free trial subscription.
- After receiving three free issues of *Financial World*, if you're still not interested in subscribing, just write "cancel" across the bill and send it back.
- *The Economist* guarantees the same free three-issue trial offer of their weekly publication.
- *In Business*, a magazine about running a more successful business will supply you with a sample issue.
- *Institutional Investor*'s family of financial and investment newsletters cost about $1,000 each for a year's subscription. You can receive a free sample issue of two of them "without cost or obligation."
- *Technical Analysis of Stocks & Commodities*, a magazine that assists traders in trading management for stocks, bonds, mutual funds, options and futures.
- *Trader's World* magazine, a magazine that features technical analysis trading techniques for stocks, bonds, options, mutual funds, and futures.
- *Comments Market Newsletter* offers a free month of weekly analysis of all markets.

What is the cost for all of these publications? Nothing. They are all free for the asking.

You may not see this many offers in your mailbox right away, but be patient. The more free things you send for, the more mailing lists your name will appear on. Yes, this does mean a lot more "junk" mail. But it also means a lot more free magazine offers, as well.

Free for as Long as You Want

The twelve Federal Reserve Banks that make up the Federal Reserve System, each publish monthly newsletters covering current business, economic, and financial matters. These newsletters, if sold as subscriptions, would be worth several hundred dollars each. They are interesting, valuable sources of information for those making decisions involving the stock market and other investments.

To receive monthly copies write to the Federal Reserve Bank in the cities listed below and request a copy of their latest newsletter. Once you have seen them all, choose which one(s) you'd like to get on a regular basis and ask to be put on their mailing list. Two of the most popular editions are those published from the St. Louis and Cleveland Banks. Other Federal Reserve Banks are located in Boston, Philadelphia, Richmond, Atlanta, Minneapolis, Chicago, New York, San Francisco, Kansas City and Dallas. This is an excellent opportunity to stay on top of financial and economic developments in this country and better understand inflation, recession and depression cycles as they occur.

What Are Magazine Discounters?

Your mailbox may also bring you packets from magazine discounters. These are mail-order companies that sell subscriptions to dozens of magazines, often (but not always) at substantial discounts. If you DO want to subscribe to a specific magazine, it may be worth your while to check out the price through one of these discounters. Their savings may range from a few cents to several dollars over the course of a subscription.

Perhaps the best known of these is Publishers' Clearing House, 382 Channel Drive, Port Washington, NY 11050. They offer a huge selection of magazines at discounts to 50 percent off the publisher's subscription rates. You may already be on their mailing list; if not, write to them and they will send you an information packet.

AMERICAN FAMILY PUBLISHERS offers similar discounts on popular magazines. You can be placed on their mailing list by writing to them at P.O. Box 6200, Tampa, FL, (800) 237-2400. Both Publishers' Clearing House and American Family Publishers have well-publicized sweepstakes contests, so not only do you get a good deal on your subscriptions, you also get a chance to win hundreds of prizes for the price of filling out the entry blanks and a single stamp.

If you are a college student or an educator, you qualify for the sizable discounts offered by AMERICAN EDUCATIONAL SERVICES, 419 Lentz Court, Lansing, MI 48917. They claim to have "the lowest educational rates anywhere." Their prices for many magazines are the lowest we have seen, and they offer a good selection of general-interest magazines as well.

MAGAZINE BUYERS' SERVICE advertises similar discounts on nationally distributed magazines. Like the others, they add no sales tax or shipping charges to your order. You pay only the fee for the subscription, which is often 50 percent less than those offered by the publishers. Write for more information at: Magazine Buyers' Service, 669 South 3rd Avenue, Mount Vernon, NY 10559, or call (203) 357-8600.

Another good opportunity for substantial discounts on your favorite publications is MAGAZINES AT DISCOUNT, P.O. Box 601, Broomall, PA 19008. Compare their prices on magazines before you subscribe elsewhere.

These companies are able to stay in business even through they offer subscriptions at less than what the magazines themselves charge for the very reason we discussed earlier: publishers need subscriptions. The advertising rates they charge are based on the size of their mailing lists. In order to add on as many subscribers as possible, they authorize these agents to sell their magazines at rates significantly below market prices.

But what if you are already subscribing to a magazine when you see it advertised for a much lower rate through a magazine discounter? No problem. By law, publishers have to refund your money for any issues they haven't already mailed, if you notify them that you want to cancel your subscription. You are then free to resubscribe at the lower rate, saving yourself money along the way. Simply write to the magazine's subscription processing address printed in the magazine, and tell them you wish to cancel your subscription and receive a refund for all unmailed issues. Remember—they are not doing you a favor here. This is the law.

Though the savings are not quite as impressive, it is also possible to buy magazines by the copy for less than the cover price. Many retail stores offer discounts off the cover price of magazines. CROWN bookstores and LUCKY supermarkets, for example, offer 10 percent discounts on all of the magazines they sell. These discounts are good bets if you don't want to invest in a subscription and haven't been offered a free copy.

If you follow our tips, you'll find that it's possible to get your favorite magazines and newsletters at a serious discount—or even for free!

GREAT DEALS ON BOOKS

Magazine publishers are not the only ones giving away free publications. We have seen hundreds of books, ours for the asking, on such diverse subjects as cooking, investing, buying car stereos, and preventing drug abuse. Everything from popular novels to maps and road atlases can be found for little effort and no money.

Chapter 5

With the price of books rising steadily year after year, even paperbacks are getting expensive. Hardcovers, needless to say, are priced even more exorbitantly. Yet full-price bookstores stay in business, largely because most people are not aware that there are alternatives. You, too, can beat the system by following our two simple rules: (1) Never pay full price for a book; and (2) Before you buy it, see if you can get it for free.

There are several sources for free books. Many businesses and manufacturers, for instance, put out books to promote themselves and their products. Food manufacturers publish hundreds of cookbooks annually, packed with thousands of recipes using ingredients that the company makes—and give the books away for free. Hotel chains and travel services give away road atlases, and may even plot your best vacation route, for free. Pharmaceutical companies offer free information on your health, diet, and general well-being. You will be amazed at the variety of free publications available from businesses and manufacturers who are trying to publicize their products or their company name.

Other prolific sources of free booklets are nonprofit foundations and trade associations. Organized to study areas of public concern or to promote their members' products or services, these groups put out numerous publications annually. We have seen books on health and disease prevention, foods, and wildlife, among many other subjects. These groups can also refer you to additional sources for in-depth information on specific diseases, for example, or particular brand names.

Literally hundreds of free books are published each year by various government agencies, as well. Most federal, state, county, and city government offices put out booklets and brochures focusing on their areas of expertise and responsibility, and will be happy to send them out to you. Look in your local telephone book's "government services" section for the appropriate department, and give them a call.

There are also government offices whose sole purpose is to publish and to distribute information to the public. The CONSUMER

INFORMATION CENTER of the U.S. GENERAL SERVICES ADMINISTRATION puts out a catalog of consumer-oriented publications several times a year. A recent issue offered 100 free or almost-free books and brochures on a wide range of subjects, including food, health, travel, and housing. For a free copy of the latest *Consumer Information Catalog*, write to the Consumer Information Center, P.O. Box 100, Pueblo, CO 81002.

A catalog listing over 700 government publications and posters is available from the U.S. SUPERINTENDENT OF DOCUMENTS. You can get this 45-page catalog by ordering item number 510W in the *Consumer Information Catalog*, or by calling your local U.S. Government Printing Office. Check the "U.S. Government" section of your phone book for their number.

Another good source for free and almost-free publications is the 42-page catalog of the COOPERATIVE EXTENSION SERVICE, Michigan State University, East Lansing, MI 48824. The catalog lists thousands of publications on subjects ranging from home furnishings to marketing to marriage.

Free Cookbooks

Manufacturers and trade associations are excellent sources for all kinds of cookbooks. Their existence depends on you, the consumer, buying their products, so it is to their benefit to help you learn new and appealing ways to use them. You may only think of buying Campbell's soup, for instance, when you want to eat soup; if CAMPBELL'S can show you how to incorporate their soups into other tasty dishes, you may buy more of it.

This reasoning encourages many manufacturers and trade associations to set up kitchens where home economists focus their efforts on creating a variety of dishes using the company's products. Because the recipes must be accessible to cooks of all levels of expertise, from novices to gourmets, each dish goes through rigorous testing and retesting to ensure consistent and nearly foolproof end results.

Chapter 5

When you request cookbooks from manufacturers and trade associations, let them know you are interested in any that they have available. Sometimes the companies will run out of particular titles, or replace them altogether with new ones. If they know that you are not set on receiving just that one title, they may send you a whole stack of booklets—all for free.

The NATIONAL PORK PRODUCERS COUNCIL will send you booklets of pork recipes for free. Two recent titles are *Pork - What a Good Idea!* and *Pork for Two*. Send a business-size, self-addressed, stamped envelope (SASE) to the National Pork Producers Council, P.O. Box 10383, Des Moines, IA 50306.

If you enjoy eating ham, you will love the dishes in *Masterpiece Ham Recipes*. Write to WILSON AND COMPANY, 4545 Lincoln Boulevard, Oklahoma City, OK 73105, for your free copy.

Traditional American Lamb Recipes is a cookbook available from the AMERICAN LAMB COUNCIL, 200 Clayton Street, Denver, CO 80206.

Sausage lovers will want to send for *Hillshire Farms Sausage Recipes*. Send your request to HILLSHIRE FARMS, Route 4, Box 227, New London, WI 54961.

Write to ZACKY FARMS, 2000 Tyler, South El Monte, CA 91733, for *Award Winning Chicken Recipes*.

The DELMARVA POULTRY INDUSTRY is offering another collection of chicken recipes, titled *Prize Winning Chicken Recipes*. Request a free copy from Delmarva Poultry Industry, R.D. 2, Box 47, Georgetown, DE 19947.

THE AMERICAN EGG BOARD, 1460 Renaissance, Park Ridge, IL 60068, is offering a cookbook full of egg recipes and basic egg-cooking techniques. For your free copy, send a business-size, self-addressed, stamped envelope (SASE) with your request.

LOUIS KEMP, a major seafood packer, has a toll-free number you can call if you would like to receive a free book of seafood recipes. Call (800) 522-1421 any weekday between the hours of 9 A.M. and 4 P.M.

A business-size, SASE will get you more seafood recipes, this time from NEW BEDFORD SEAFOOD. Write to them at P.O. Box 307, Fair Haven, MA 02719 for your free copy.

The MAINE DEPARTMENT OF MARINE RESOURCES, State House, Augusta, ME 04333, has free cookbooks with recipes using New England seafood.

Soups, casseroles, sandwiches—even pizza—can be made with sloppy-joe sauce. Write to MANWICH for *Dinnertime Dramas*, P.O. Box 8581/GH, Clinton, Iowa 52736.

A collection of salmon and crab recipes is available from EVANS/PACIFIC, INC. Write to them at 300 Elliot Avenue, West Seattle, WA 98119, for their free cookbook.

Halibut lovers will want this book of recipes using their favorite fish. Ask for halibut recipes from the HALIBUT ASSOCIATION OF NORTH AMERICA, 309 Maritime Building, 911 Western Avenue, Seattle, WA 98104.

HORMEL, P.O. Box 5002, Austin, MN 55912, has recipes using Hormel's canned meats and salmon. These dishes use canned chunk chicken, turkey, ham, and salmon—great pantry staples for quick, nutritious family meals.

More quick recipes are available in BISQUICK'S *No Time to Cook* book, using Bisquick's buttermilk baking mix. Send for a free copy from Bisquick *No Time to Cook,* P.O. Box 1112, Department 90, Minneapolis, MN 55440.

THE RICE COUNCIL is a good source for recipes using rice as a main ingredient. Write to them for their free collection of recipes at P.O. Box 740121, Houston, TX 77274.

UNCLE BEN'S also offers a free rice recipe booklet. You can request it from Uncle Ben's Recipe Booklet, P.O. Box 11877, Chicago, IL 60611. Write to Uncle Ben's Country Inn Recipes, P.O. Box 11166, Chicago, IL 60611.

Authentic Italian Pasta Recipes is a collection of 20 pasta recipes that is yours for the asking. Request this booklet from RAGU FOODS, INC., 33 Benedict Place, Greenwich, CT 06830.

Chapter 5

More noodle recipes are available from NISSIN FOODS, makers of oriental-style noodles. Write to Nissin Foods, Department O, Gardena, CA 90249, and they will send them to you.

The *Perfect Couscous Recipe Collection* is being offered by NEAR EAST FOOD PRODUCTS, P.O. Box 1227, Boston, MA 02277-1227. Send them your name and address for a free copy.

A collection of bran-rich dishes has been put together for those trying to increase their intake of dietary fiber. A free copy is yours for the asking by writing to Bran Recipes, P.O. Box 853, Young America, MN 55399.

The home economists at KELLOGG'S have several booklets available which use their company's breakfast cereals as ingredients, including *Kellogg's Cereal Recipe Collection* and the *Kids-Can-Do-It* cookbook. Request them from the Department of Home Economic Services, Kellogg Company, 1 Kellogg Square, Battle Creek, MI 49016.

Rice cakes, those light rounds of puffed rice, are the subject of CHICO-SAN's cookbook. Write for a free copy from Chico-San Recipe Book, P.O. Box 1055, Boston, MA 02277-1055.

AMERICAN POPCORN COMPANY, P.O. Box 178, Sioux City, IA 51102, has put together a book of recipes using popcorn. When you write to them, ask for a copy of *Favorite Popcorn Recipes*.

A collection of recipes using bread (not bread-baking recipes) is available from ROMAN MEAL COMPANY. Send for your free copy of *Roman Recipe Collection* from Roman Meal Company, P.O. Box 11126, Tacoma, WA 98411.

Quaker's Best Recipes is a cookbook put together by the QUAKER OATS COMPANY. Write to them at Merchandise Mart Plaza, Chicago, IL 60654, for a free copy.

The agricultural industry puts out many cookbooks using everything from fruit and fruit juices to vegetables and nuts. For tips and recipes for Idaho potatoes, ask the IDAHO POTATO COMMISSION for *Idaho Potato Tips and Recipes*. Their address is P.O. Box 1068, Boise, ID 83701.

Sweet potatoes are the subject of a free recipe collection offered by the LOUISIANA SWEET POTATO COMMISSION. Write to them at P.O. Box 113, Opelousas, LA 70570, and they will send it out.

Dried peas and lentils are good sources of protein and are very economical. A packet of recipe cards and cookbooks using these products is available for free from the Washington and Idaho DRY PEA AND LENTIL COMMISSIONS, P.O. Box 8566, Moscow, ID 83843.

Recipes for Mushroom Lovers is a booklet of recipes using—you guessed it—mushrooms. Request your copy from the AMERICAN MUSHROOM INSTITUTE, P.O. Box 373, Kennett Square, PA 19348.

Salads, soups, and stews are among the dishes in *Veg-All Recipes*. Get a free copy of this booklet by writing to VEG-ALL Recipes, LARSEN COMPANY, P.O. Box 190265, Green Bay, WI 54307-9026.

Apricots, both fresh and dried, are the subject of a recipe collection from the CALIFORNIA APRICOT ADVISORY BOARD. Write to them at 1280 Boulevard Way, Suite 107, Walnut Creek, CA 94595.

Recipes using juicy Florida citrus fruit are available from that state's DEPARTMENT OF CITRUS. Send for this free booklet from the State of Florida, Department of Citrus, P.O. Box 148, Lakeland, FL 33802.

More citrus recipes are available, this time from TEXASWEET. Ask for "TexaSweet Citrus Recipes" when you write to TexaSweet, P.O. Box 2497, McAllen, TX 78501.

Write to the CALIFORNIA STRAWBERRY ADVISORY BOARD, P.O. Box 269, Watsonville, CA 95077, and request their strawberry recipe booklet.

Fruits of Summer contains recipes and suggestions for using plums, peaches, nectarines, and other summer fruits, and helpful tips on home canning. You can get a free copy by writing to the CALIFORNIA TREE FRUIT AGREEMENT, P.O. Box 255383, Sacramento, CA 95825.

Who knows apples better than the WASHINGTON STATE APPLE COMMISSION? A collection of their best recipes is available if you write to them at P.O. Box 18, Wenatchee, WA 98801. Ask for "Recipes with Apples."

For a collection of recipes using DOLE's canned pineapple, write to "Dole's Quick and Easy Recipes," P.O. Box 7758, San Francisco, CA 94120. Include a business-size SASE.

More recipes, this time using apple cider, are available from S. MARTINELLI AND COMPANY, P.O. Box 549, Watsonville, CA 95077. When you write, ask for Martinelli's Cider Recipes.

Citrus juices are the featured ingredient in TREESWEET PRODUCTS' recipe collection. For a free copy, write to Treesweet Products, P.O. Box 28, Santa Ana, CA 92702.

Sun-Maid raisins star in the recipes developed by SUN-MAID RAISIN GROWERS OF CALIFORNIA, Kingsburg, CA 93631. They will be happy to send you a free copy of their cookbook.

For still more raisin recipes write to the CALIFORNIA RAISIN ADVISORY BOARD, P.O. Box 5335, Fresno, CA 93755, for a copy of their booklet.

Prunes are featured in a cookbook full of great ways to increase fiber in your diet painlessly. Send for a free copy from PRUNE IDEAS, P.O. Box 882168, San Francisco, CA 94188-2168.

THE DRIED FRUIT ADVISORY BOARD, P.O. Box 709, Fresno, CA 93712, can send you recipes that they have developed, too. Their free collection features apricots, raisins, and other varieties of plump dried fruit.

Nut lovers will enjoy this collection of favorite almond recipes called *A Collection of Almond Recipe Favorites*, from the ALMOND BOARD OF CALIFORNIA, P.O. Box 15920, Sacramento, CA 95852.

You'll also want to send for a free copy of the *Macadamia Gazette*. It's packed with recipes using crunchy macadamia nuts. Write to MAUNA LOA MACADAMIA NUT CORPORATION, S.P. Box 3, Volcano Highway, Hilo, HI 96720.

The dairy industry is always coming up with creative new ways to use dairy products. The makers of VELVEETA have pulled together some favorite recipes using their popular processed cheese. Send for a free copy from Velveeta Cookbook, P.O. Box 833, South Holland, IL 60473.

Cooking with Casino is another great collection of cheese recipes. Write to CASINO CHEESE Recipes, P.O. Box 841, South Holland, IL 60473.

FRIGO CHEESE CORPORATION, manufacturers of mozzarella, ricotta, and other cheeses, also has a free cookbook out. Write to them at P.O. Box 19024, Department C, Green Bay, WI 54307-9024.

GERBER CHEESE COMPANY, INC., has a toll-free consumer hotline with helpful messages concerning their Swiss Knight Gruyere cheese wedges. The 24-hour hotline number is (800) SO-SWISS. Call and you can hear recipes and nutritional information, updated regularly, for free.

Favorite Yogurt Recipes from Dannon is available from Yogurt Recipes, DANNON COMPANY, 22-11 38th Avenue, Long Island City, NY 11101.

Another great collection of yogurt recipes has been published by CONTINENTAL YOGURT, 1358 East Colorado Street, Glendale, CA 91206. Request *Yummy Recipes Made with Yummy Yogurt.*

Milk-Free Recipes is aimed at the millions of people who can't drink milk or eat anything made with it. If that sounds like you, you'll want these free recipes. Write to Educational Services, ROSS LABORATORIES, Columbus, OH 43216.

Soy milk is a substitute you may also want to consider if you suffer from a milk allergy. MEAD JOHNSON has designed several menus using this product. Request *Meals Without Milk* from Prosobee, Mead Johnson, Evansville, IN 47721.

Soy sauce is the subject of SAN-J's cookbook. Featuring their Tamari soy sauce, it is available for free by writing to San-J, Department B, 2880 Sprouse Drive, Richmond, VA 23231.

Chapter 5

The *Kikkoman Recipe Collection* uses soy sauce and Teriyaki to make dishes taste great. Get a free copy of this booklet from KIKKOMAN INTERNATIONAL, P.O. Box 784, San Francisco, CA 94101.

If spicy-hot is more your style, how about a book of recipes using Tabasco sauce? *From the Land of Tabasco Sauce* is available from McILHENNY COMPANY, Avery Island, LA 70513.

More "hot" ideas are featured in *Seasoning with Trappey's Red Devil Hot Sauce.* Write to B.F. TRAPPEY'S SONS, Drawer 400, New Iberia, LA 70560. Also ask for a copy of *Trappey's and Sugary Sam's Yam Recipes*—it's also free.

Fans of Worcestershire sauce will want the recipes developed by LEA AND PERRINS. Request a free copy of *Recipes with Worcestershire* from Lea and Perrins, Fairlawn, NJ 07410.

We are all familiar with those old standby seasonings, salt and pepper. HEUBLEIN, INC., makers of Dijon mustard, has put out a free book of recipes using what they call *The Third Seasoning.* Write to Heublein, Inc., Farmington, CT 06032.

Spice up your cooking with a free spice and herb chart. Send a business-size SASE Consumer Services Department, MC-CORMICK AND COMPANY, INC., 414 Light Street, Baltimore, MD 21202.

More advice on seasonings is available from R.T. FRENCH COMPANY, Rochester, NY 14609. Write to them and request a free copy of their *Wonderful World of Seasoning* chart. It will clear up a lot of guesswork when it comes to creative cooking.

A collection of recipes using their products has been developed by GOYA'S SEASONINGS. Send for it by writing to Goya Recipes, Secaucus, NJ 07094.

Another collection of recipes, this time featuring seasoned salt, is available from LAWRY'S, Department SS, P.O. Box 2572, Los Angeles, CA 90051. Request their Lawry's Seasoned Salt recipes.

Dinnertime Dramas is one of the most entertaining cookbooks around. It incorporates 26 recipes using MANWICH Sloppy Joe sauce into a mystery story. Fun for both kids and adults, it's free from Manwich Dinnertime Dramas, P.O. Box 8581, Clinton, IA 52736.

Two booklets of horseradish recipes have been published for those who are interested in novel ways to use this unique condiment. The first is by GOLD'S, 9057 McDonald Avenue, Brooklyn, NY 11218.

The second booklet is free from MOREHOUSE FOODS, 4221 Hollis, Emeryville, CA 94608. Ask for their free horseradish recipes.

We all love Chinese food, but rarely recreate our favorite restaurant dishes at home. La Choy has put together a free collection of Chinese recipes. Write to La Choy, Archibald, OH 43502.

More favorite recipes are available from AMSTAR, INC., P.O. Box 625, New York, NY 10036. *America's Regional Favorites* includes everything from main dishes to desserts, and covers all types of American ethnic and regional cuisines.

Favorite French Recipes features dishes from one of the world's finest cuisines. This booklet has been put together by AIR FRANCE, 1350 Avenue of the Americas, New York, NY 10019.

Over 100 recipes for Canadian dishes are available in the *Canadian Recipe Collection.* Send for a free copy from CANADA DEPARTMENT OF AGRICULTURE, Ottawa, Canada K1A 0C7.

A business-size SASE will get you a free copy of *Food Secrets of Mexico*, a collection of Mexican recipes designed to wake up your taste buds. Write to LA VICTORIA RECIPES, P.O. Box 3884, City of Industry, CA 91744.

Another booklet of Mexican food recipes is available for free from EL RIO MEXICAN FOODS, P.O. Box 38, Dayton, OH 45449.

Many of the above books include recipes for desserts and sweets. But there are also quite a few free books that are entirely devoted to satisfying your sweet tooth. JELLY BELLY jellybeans has a collection of recipes for baking with jellybeans. Call Jelly Belly any weekday between 9 A.M. and 5 P.M. Eastern Standard Time, at (800) JBBEANS, and they will send you a free copy.

C & H SUGAR has several free booklets of cookie and dessert recipes. Send a business-size, SASE to C & H Sugar Kitchen, 1390 Willow Pass Road, Concord, CA 94520, and request *Powdered Sugar Cookies*, featuring cookies made with powdered sugar, Bar Cookies, or *From Our Private Collection*.

Chocoholics will want to send or call for HERSHEY'S chocolate cookbooks. Current titles, available for free, are *Hershey's Favorite Recipes*, *Hershey's Cocoa Recipes*, *Hershey's Chocolate Chip Recipes*, and *Reese's Peanut Butter Chip Recipes*. Call Hershey Foods at (800) 468-1714 any weekday, between 9 A.M. and 4 P.M. Eastern Standard Time, or write to Consumer Information, Hershey Foods, 19 East Chocolate Avenue, Hershey, PA 17033.

NESTLÉ also offers many free cookbooks to chocolate lovers. Request copies of all of their current titles from Nestlé Test Kitchen, 100 Bloomingdale Road, White Plains, NY 10605.

Dieters with sweet teeth will love *Reduced Fat Goodies*, a collection of low-fat desserts made with safflower oil. Send a business-size, SASE to SAFFLOWER INFORMATION BUREAU, 928 Broadway, New York, NY 10010.

If you love pies, but dread their time-consuming preparation, try Lucky Leaf pie fillings' shortcuts. KNOUSE FOODS, Peach Glen, PA 17306, offers a cookbook called *Good So Many Ways*, featuring their prepared pie filling. Best of all, it's free.

Recipes for Something Special contains recipes using maraschino cherries and other canned fruits. You can get this booklet for free from LIBERTY CHERRY AND FRUIT COMPANY, 227 West Southern Avenue, Covington, KY 41015.

For desserts with a bit more of a kick, send for *Adventures in Taste with VANDERMINT Imported Liqueur*. You'll get a great assortment of dessert and drink recipes that use Vandermint chocolate-mint liqueur. Send for your free copy from Vandermint Recipes, P.O. Box 729, Bardstown, KY 40004.

Write to KAHLUA, Department A, P.O. Box 230, Los Angeles, CA 90078-0230, for a free booklet of recipes made with Kahlua coffee liqueur. The *Kahlua Recipe Book* contains not only drink and dessert recipes, but also many for main and side dishes, all flavored with coffee liqueur.

Drambuie Recipe Book has drink and other recipes which use Drambuie liqueur. For a free copy, write to W.A. TAYLOR AND COMPANY, 501 Brickell Key Drive, Miami, FL 33131.

HIRAM WALKER, P.O. Box 33006, Detroit, MI 48232, is offering a booklet featuring innovative and old-fashioned uses for their many cordials. Ask them for a free copy of *Cordial Recipes*.

More cordial recipes are available in *The Cordial Life*, a free booklet published by NATIONAL DISTILLERS PRODUCTS COMPANY, 99 Park Avenue, New York, NY 10016.

A booklet of dishes calling for Chambord raspberry liqueur has been published by LA MAISON DELAN ET CIE. Ask for a free copy of *Chambord Recipes* when you write to Chambord Recipes, La Maison Delan et Cie., 2180 Oakdale Drive, Philadelphia, PA 19125.

Wine is a common ingredient in dishes from many cuisines, and its versatility is reflected in the many cookbooks available on the subject. *Cooking with Wine* is one such cookbook, featuring many dishes in which wine is used. A free copy is yours for writing to PAUL MASSON VINEYARDS, P.O. Box 2279, Saratoga, CA 95070.

Another collection of recipes calling for wine is available from the E & J GALLO WINERY. Request *Gallo Wine and Dine* from E & J Gallo Winery, Modesto, CA 95353.

Creative Cooking with Taylor Wines is also full of wine-flavored dishes. For this free recipe collection, write to TAYLOR WINE COMPANY, Hammondsport, NY 14840.

The makers of Almaden wines are offering a collection of recipes they have developed in their kitchens. Request *Almaden Recipes* when you write to ALMADEN VINEYARDS, 1530 Blossom Road, San Jose, CA 95118.

Cooking with Sherry is a good source of recipes that use, yes, sherry. Get your free copy from the SHERRY INSTITUTE OF SPAIN, 220 East 42nd Street, New York, NY 10017.

Chapter 5

With so many recipes for wine, many of us don't even think of cooking with its more humble relative, beer. *Favorite Recipes with Beer* will change that. Write to the U.S. BREWERS ASSOCIATION, Inc. 1750 "K" Street Northwest, Washington, DC 20006, and they will send it to you for free.

The CALIFORNIA HONEY ADVISORY BOARD has a free booklet available that features the golden nectar, honey. Write for *Honey Recipes*, California Honey Advisory Board, P.O. Box 265, Sonoma, CA 95476.

Cook It Right with Honey is another great collection of honey recipes. Send for a free copy from DADANT AND SONS, Hamilton, IL 62341.

The SIOUX HONEY ASSOCIATION has put together an assortment of their favorite honey recipes, called *Honey Magic*. Get a free copy of this booklet from them at P.O. Box 388, Sioux City, IA 51102.

Many of the major food companies produce wide varieties of items and cookbooks that reflect variety. The *Best Foods Recipe Collection*, for instance, offers recipes using Hellman's and Best Foods mayonnaise, Mazola corn oil, Karo corn syrup, and Skippy peanut butter. This cookbook is available for free from BEST FOODS, Consumer Services Department, International Plaza, Englewood, NY 07632.

Tomatoes, beans, and fruit are among S & W's products, and are featured in their cookbook. For your free copy, write to S & W FINE FOODS, Consumer Services, P.O. 5580, San Mateo, CA 94402.

You can get a collection of recipes that use LIBBY, MCNEIL & LIBBY products by sending a note to Home Economics Department, 1800 West 119th Street, Chicago, IL 60643. Ask for a free copy of *Kitchen-Tested Recipes*.

A variety of recipes are available from the PURE FOOD COMPANY, INC., Department V, Mamaroneck, NY 10543.

That Special Touch is a collection of recipes developed in the BETTY CROCKER KITCHENS. Request your free copy from

GENERAL MILLS, Betty Crocker Kitchens, P.O. Box 1113, Minneapolis, MN 55440.

Durkee produces all sorts of foods, including French-fried onions, packaged coconut, and spices. The *Durkee Famous Recipe Collection*, shows you how to use these ingredients and more. Write to DURKEE FAMOUS FOODS, 24600 Center Ridge Road, Westlake, OH 44145.

NABISCO has an extensive collection of recipes, including *Recipes for Holiday Entertaining*. Request their test kitchen recipe books. Write to Nabisco, Home Economics Department, East Hanover, NJ 07936.

Dole and Bumble Bee are just two of the brands owned by CASTLE AND COOKE FOODS, P.O. Box 7330, San Francisco, CA 94120. Ask for the *Castle and Cooke Recipe Collection."*

PILLSBURY COMPANY, P.O. Box 5819, Minneapolis, MN 55460, has a recipe booklet featuring many familiar Pillsbury products, used in new ways. When you write, also request *Creative Cooking from Hungry Jack*, for recipes using instant mashed potatoes and pancake mix.

A business-size, SASE will get you a free book of recipes using CAMPBELL'S soups. Request the *Campbell's Soup Recipe Book,* from Campbell's, P.O. Box 1232, Bensalam, PA 19020.

Heinz Recipe Collection is a free booklet by H.J. HEINZ, which features Heinz's products in many different dishes. They also offer a booklet called *Heinz Cooking with Beans.* For copies write to H.J. Heinz, P.O. Box 57, Philadelphia, PA 15230.

Stretching Food Dollars is a booklet offered by QUAKER to help you cut your food budget painlessly. Request one from Quaker *Stretching Food Dollars* Offer, P.O. Box 11257, Chicago, IL 60611.

Call or write to JIM BEAM for a copy of their free booklet on entertaining. Call (800) 74JBEAM or send your name and address to *Entertaining at Home: An American Basic*, c/o Jim Beam, 510 Lake Cook Road, Deerfield, IL 60015.

Recipes and helpful hints are yours free in the U.S. Department of Agriculture's Bulletin number 370, titled *Cooking for Small Groups*. Write to the U.S. Department of Agriculture, Publications Division, Washington, DC 20250.

Write to FIELD PUBLICATIONS, 4343 Equity Drive, P.O. Box 16689, Columbus, OH 43216, for information on their McCall's Cooking School offer. They will send you information on how to get 36 free recipe cards and a three-ring binder, with no obligation to buy anything else. You can cancel your membership with the program immediately, and end up paying nothing.

Free Crafts Books

If your creativity runs more towards crafting than cooking, you will be delighted with the number of free crafts books and patterns you can get. Offered by manufacturers and publishers of crafts magazines and books, these projects will keep your fingers busy. Materials are all you will have to pay for.

RIT DYE will send you instructions on how to dye wood and wicker furniture and a dye color chart. Write to *Wood and Wicker Colorworks* Booklet, Rit Dye, Department 162, P.O. Box 2932, Young America, MN 55399-2932.

Dyeing fabrics is the subject of *The Art of Color Dyeing*. It covers dyeing by hand and washing machine, tie dyeing and batik. Send your name and address to *The Art of Color Dyeing*, P.O. Box 307, Coventry, CT 06238.

A business-size, SASE will get you crochet patterns for a variety of charming animal puppet mittens. Write to *Animal Puppet Mittens Pattern*, Lorraine Vetter, 7924-AP Soper Hill Road, Everett, WA 98205.

A ribbons and lace barrette pattern is available from KIMDEE PRODUCTS, 2014 Ridgecrest Drive, Knoxville, TN 37918. Enclose a business-size SASE with your request.

ARM & HAMMER will send you free instructions on how to make a fire pail to keep by the stove, and a fire pail label. Send a business-size, SASE to Fire Pail Label, ARM & HAMMER DIVISION, CHURCH & DWIGHT COMPANY, INC., P.O. Box 7648-N, Princeton, NJ 08543-7648.

Instructions and a pattern to knit a gingerbread boy ornament are offered by Hazelcrafts. Send a business-size SASE to *Easy Knitted Gingerbread Boy Ornament*, HAZELCRAFTS, P.O. Box 175, Woburn, MA 01801.

Information on jewelry-making, including stamping, antiquing, etching, and embossing, is available in a free book called *Copper Handicraft*. Write to COPPER DEVELOPMENT ASSOCIATION, Greenwich Office Park 2, P.O. Box 1840, Greenwich, CT 06836.

Paper crafts are the subject of a free book available if you send a business-size SASE to HOBBY INDUSTRY OF AMERICA, 319 East 54th Street, Elmwood Park, NJ 07407. You'll get information on origami, decoupage, quilling, sculpture, and more.

The makers of Handi Wrap And Ziploc bags have a booklet that outlines projects you can do using their products. Write to *Craft Magic*, DOW CHEMICAL COMPANY, Consumer Products, P.O. Box 68511, Indianapolis, IN 46268. Also request their *Fun With Styrofoam* booklets.

Dow also has a book called *The Crafty Creations Pattern Book*, which has instructions for making a bird feeder, dolls, pencil holders, etc. Write to DOW CONSUMER PRODUCTS, Texise Division, Consumer Affairs Department, P.O. Box 368, Greenville, SC 29602-0368.

A recipe for making "play clay" out of baking soda is available by writing to *Play Clay*, Arm & Hammer, P.O. Box 369, Piscataway, NJ 08854. They will also send instructions for making gifts, decorations, and jewelry.

Elmer's glue can be used to make clay and paint. A business-size SASE will get you instructions and ideas for puppets, magnets, and other projects. Contact Consumer Products Division, BORDEN CHEMICAL, 180 East Broad Street, Columbus, OH 43215, and ask for *Mix 'n' Make—Glue Dough—Glue Paint*.

Chapter 5

A free booklet called *How You Can Make Paper* is available from the AMERICAN PAPER INSTITUTE, INC., 260 Madison Avenue, New York, NY 10016.

Free Hobby Books

Free books on hobbies are always available, if you know where to get them. The AMERICAN PHILATELIC SOCIETY, P.O. Box 800, State College, PA 16801, offers a booklet called *How to Organize a Stamp Club*.

Another book on stamp collecting, including selection and what they represent, is available from the U.S. POSTAL SERVICE, Philatelic Sales Division, Washington, D.C. 20265. Request their *Philatelic Catalog*.

Beginning stamp collectors may be interested in *How to Collect Stamps*. Write to LITTLETON/MYSTIC STAMP COMPANY, 96 Main Street, Camden, NY 13316.

If you are a coin collector *Numismatic News Weekly* will send you a free copy of their publication. Write to NUMISMATIC NEWS WEEKLY, Iola, WI 54990.

Tell them you collect coins and the AMERICAN NUMISMATIC ASSOCIATION will send you a 240-page book called *The Numismatist*. This book covers collecting coins, paper money, tokens, and medals. Write to *The Numismatist*, American Numismatic Association, P.O. Box 2366, Colorado Springs, CO 80903.

The NATIONAL CARD COLLECTING ASSOCIATION, P.O. Box 573, Wayne City, IL 62895, will send you free information on collecting baseball cards.

Let's Collect Shells and Rocks is the title of a book available from SHELL OIL COMPANY, Public Affairs Department, Room 1535, P.O. Box 2463, Houston, TX 77001.

Sample track layouts and help on setting them up are available in *Introduction to Scale Model Railroading*. It's available for free from KALMBACH PUBLISHING COMPANY, 1027 North 7th Street, Milwaukee, WI 53233.

Roman Gothic, Old English, and Manuscript lettering charts and hints on calligraphy are available for free by writing to HUNT BIENFANG PAPER COMPANY, 2020 West Front Street, Statesville, NC 28677.

Free instructions on how to perform a magic trick, for novice or expert magicians, is available if you send a business-size SASE to *Magic Trick*, SORCERER MAGIC, 10 Lincoln Avenue, Saint Albans, VT 05478.

Amateur photographers can get three booklets on picture-taking from the EASTMAN KODAK COMPANY, 343 State Street, Rochester, NY 14650. Ask them for *Picture Taking: A Self-Teaching Guide*, *Tips for Better Pictures*, and *Picture Taking in Five Minutes*. They also have a booklet called *How to Make and Use a Pinhole Camera*, which tells how to turn a box or a can into a working camera.

Beginning chess players will find chess basics in *How Do You Play Chess?*, free from DOVER PUBLICATIONS, INC., 180 Varick Street, New York, NY 10014.

More chess tips are available if you send a business-size, SASE to the U.S. CHESS FEDERATION, 186 Route 9W, New Windsor, NY 12550. Ask for *Ten Tips to Winning Chess*.

Free Sports and Games Books

There is no need to pay high membership fees at gyms and health clubs; all the information you need to stay fit and in shape is available for free. Running is one way to exercise for next-to-nothing, and *Cold Weather Running* is a solid source of advice on running in cold weather, including tips on training and spotting hazards. Write to the AMERICAN RUNNING AND FITNESS ASSOCIATION, 9310 Old Georgetown Road, Bethesda, MD 20814.

The L'eggs Women Runner's Guide is a free booklet that provides warm-up tips and a running diary. Write to L'eggs Running Program, L'EGGS HOSIERY, P.O. Box 2495, Winston-Salem, NC 27102.

Several free publications on fitness are available from the PRESIDENT'S COUNCIL ON PHYSICAL FITNESS, DEPARTMENT OF HEALTH AND HUMAN SERVICES, 450 5th Street, Suite 7103, Washington, D.C. 20001. Write to them and request a listing or call them at (202) 272-3430.

A guide to stretching, warm-ups, and exercising is available from OCCIDENTAL LIFE INSURANCE COMPANY OF CALIFORNIA, P.O. Box 2101 Terminal Annex, Los Angeles, CA 90051. Ask them for *Exercise Your Right to Live.*

The New Guide to Year Round Fitness for Everyone tells how to look and feel better in just 10 to 15 minutes each day. Write to the TEA COUNCIL OF THE U.S., 230 Park Avenue, New York, NY 10169.

How to Roller Skate and *Fun and Games on Roller Skates* are available for free from CHICAGO ROLLER SKATE COMPANY, 4458 West Lake Street, Chicago, IL 60424. You'll find out how to stroke, steer, and stop, and do turns, tricks, and spins.

AETNA, 151 Farmington Avenue, Hartford, CT 06156, is offering a booklet called *Bicycle Safety*, to help keep you on the road and out of trouble. Ask them for their *Play It Safe* coloring book and *Save Your Child from Poisoning*, also available for free.

Cycling Safety Rules is another publication for bicyclists. Write to EMPLOYERS INSURANCE OF WAUSAU, Safety and Health Services Department, Wausau, WI 54401.

Two books for bowlers are being offered by AMF BOWLING PRODUCTS, Public Affairs Department, P.O. Box 31640, Richmond, VA 23294-1640. Ask for *Bowling Tips* and *Hints on Improving Your Bowling Score.*

Beginning bowlers, no matter how old, can learn from *Tips for Young Bowlers*, a free booklet available by sending a business-size SASE to the AMERICAN BOWLER'S ASSOCIATION, 5301 South 76th Street, Greendale, WI 53129.

Bowling Fundamentals, is a free booklet that has illustrated step-by-step instructions and an explanation of bowling etiquette. Write to YOUNG AMERICAN BOWLING ALLIANCE, 5301 South 76th Street, Greendale, WI 53129.

Horseshoe pitching may not be the best exercise, but it can be fun. *Horseshoe Pitching Rules* is available for free from the NATIONAL ASSOCIATION OF HORSESHOE PITCHERS, c/o *Horseshoe Pitcher's News Digest*, 1307 Solfisburg Avenue, Aurora, IL 60505.

Kids and kids-at-heart will enjoy a pamphlet called *Yo-Yo Tricks* from the makers of yo-yos, DUNCAN TOYS COMPANY, P.O. Box 165, Baraboo, WI 53913. Send a business-size SASE with your request.

Water skiers should send for *The Guide to Safe Water Skiing* offered by the AMERICAN WATER SKIING ASSOCIATION, 799 Overlook Drive, Winter Haven, FL 33884. Send a business-size SASE with your request.

The AMERICAN ATHLETIC UNION, Order Department, 3400 West 86th Street, Indianapolis, IN 46268, has several books available on all sports. Ask for *The AAU Junior Olympic Guide*, a 104-page book covering 15 different sports and official rules, The AAU's Physical Fitness Program, and AAU Scoring Tables.

Team Up for Fitness offers a fun physical education program geared toward kids. Send a business-size SASE to Jim Johnson, HERSHEY YOUTH PROGRAM, P.O. Box 814, Hershey, PA 17033-0814.

Outdoors enthusiasts will want the free backpacking and camping guide called *Backpacking with Ease*. Write to DOW CHEMICAL COMPANY, Consumer Products Division, P.O. Box 68511, Indianapolis, IN 46268.

Maps of bicycling and hiking trails throughout the National Park Service are available from the U.S. DEPARTMENT OF THE

INTERIOR, 18th and C Streets Northwest, Room 1013, Washington, D.C. 20240.

Facts About Federal Wildlife Laws, available from the U.S. DEPARTMENT OF THE INTERIOR, FISH AND WILDLIFE SERVICE, Washington, D.C. 20240, will tell you about hunting rules and where to get hunting permits.

CISCO KID TACKLE, INC., 2630 Northwest 1st Avenue, Boca Raton, FL 33431, is offering a free booklet titled *Fishing Tips*.

Basketball players and armchair athletes alike will enjoy *Basketball Was Born Here*, on the history of basketball. Send a business-size SASE to BASKETBALL HALL OF FAME, P.O. Box 175, Highland Station, Springfield, MA 01109.

The Olympic Games covers the history of the Olympics, from their founding in 776 B.C. to the present. Write to the U.S. OLYMPIC COMMITTEE, 1750 East Boulder Street, Colorado Springs, CO 80909.

Free Travel Books

Before you plan your next vacation, get as much information as you can on the places you're considering visiting. State offices of tourism have excellent free booklets, calendars, and maps available to prospective visitors. Call directory assistance for the state in which you are interested for the number of the State Office of Tourism.

Similar information is available on an international level by contacting a country's U.S. embassy or tourist office. THE EGYPT TOURIST AUTHORITY, for instance, will send free information on Egypt, including a chart of the hieroglyphic alphabet, if you write to them at 630 5th Avenue, New York, NY 10111.

Tips on traveling alone are available if you send a business-size SASE to PARTNERS-IN-TRAVEL, P.O. Box 491145, Los Angeles, CA 90049. Ask for *Sure-Fire Tips for Successful Solo Travel*.

Destination Good Health: A Guide to Healthy Travel Habits includes information on exercise, nutrition, and foot care for travelers. For a free copy, write to THE ROCKPORT COMPANY, Attention: Travel Brochure, 72 Howe Street, Marlboro, MA 01752.

To help make traveling with children a good experience, send for the *Children's Discovery Kit*, a packet of materials including a color map of the U.S., a travel planner, a geography learning guide, and more. Write to FREE CHILDREN'S DISCOVERY KIT OFFER, P.O. Box 513, Department P, Gibbstown, NJ 08027.

The Best Western hotel chain is offering a free *Road Atlas* and *Travel Guide*. Write to BEST WESTERN, INC., P.O. Box 10203, Phoenix, AZ 85064.

Free road maps are available from TEXACO TRAVEL SERVICE, P.O. Box 1459, Houston, TX 77001. If you tell them your travel plans, they will outline your best route for no charge.

Members of the AMERICAN AUTOMOBILE ASSOCIATION (AAA) can stop by any office for free local and long-distance maps and route advice. They will also help you plan your trip.

NORTHWESTERN MUTUAL LIFE INSURANCE COMPANY, 720 East Wisconsin Avenue, Milwaukee, WI 53202, recently offered a free copy of the latest *Rand McNally Road Atlas* along with information on their life insurance.

Music to Your Ears

A collection of Christmas carols is available for free from your local John Hancock agent or by writing to JOHN HANCOCK MUTUAL LIFE INSURANCE, P.O. Box 111, Boston, MA 02117.

Wind instruments are the subject of four booklets offered by SELMER, Elkhart, IN 46516. These free booklets are called *Clarinets*, *Saxophones*, *Flutes and Piccolos*, and *Oboes and Bassoons*.

How to Play the Hohner Harmonica offers a step-by-step guide and a song book, and tells you how to create special effects. From M. HOHNER, INC., P.O. Box 15035, Richmond, VA 23227.

How Music Can Bring You Closer to Your Child is a free booklet available from G. LEBLANC CORPORATION, 7019 30th Avenue, Kenosha, WI 53141. It offers help to parents who want to get their children interested in playing a musical instrument.

For Kids and Parents

Raising children in this complicated world is not easy. Here are some free publications that can help make it a bit easier:

The NATIONAL COUNCIL OF TEACHERS OF ENGLISH, 1111 Kenyon Road, Urbana, IL 61801, is offering a free booklet called *How to Help Your Child Become a Better Writer,* available in English or Spanish. Send a business-size SASE with your request.

More writing tips are available in *Write with Style* and *How to Write Clearly*. They are available from INTERNATIONAL PAPER COMPANY, P.O. Box 954, Madison Square Station, New York, NY 10010.

Parents of teenagers should send for this free booklet on safe driving. Called *Tips for Teen-Age Drivers*, it's available from FIRESTONE TIRE AND RUBBER COMPANY, Educational Services Bureau, Akron, OH 44317.

Super Sitter contains tips and hints for teens who babysit for extra money. Write to the U.S. CONSUMER PRODUCT SAFETY COMMISSION, Washington, DC 20207, and request booklet number 052-011-00114-7.

Get your children involved with what goes on in the kitchen with the *Bake-a-Bread Book for Beginners*, available free from FLEISHMANN'S EDUCATIONAL SERVICES DEPARTMENT, P.O. Box 2695, Grand Central Station, New York, NY 10017.

Party Game Ideas is a lifesaver for parents who need to plan kids' parties. Send a business-size SASE to PARTY CREATIONS, R.D. 2, Box 35, Red Hook, NY 12571.

Another source of party game ideas is *Let's Make a Bubble Gum Party*. Write to Topps Chewing Gum Company, P.O. Box 300, Westbury, NY 11590.

If your son or daughter is in high school, and is anticipating that first year at college, send for *How to Survive Freshman Year.* It's free from Loyola University of Chicago, 820 North Michigan Avenue, Suite 1500, Chicago, IL 60611.

Also send for "I Wish I'd Known That Before I Came to College," from *Wish I'd Known*, Department KC, UNIVERSITY OF ROCHESTER, Rochester, NY 14627. Send a business-size SASE with your request.

Another useful guide to coping with college is titled *Facing Facts About Your College Career*. It's free from PRUDENTIAL INSURANCE COMPANY, Public Relations Department, P.O. Box 141, Boston, MA 02199.

Et Cetera

By now you probably realize that you can get information on whatever you're interested in for free. Much of the information in these booklets is even more up to date than what you'd find in an encyclopedia, because lower printing costs enable companies and organizations to keep the booklets current. Particularly useful for families with school-age children, the following sources offer information on a wide variety of topics.

A free sign language alphabet card is available from KEEP QUIET, P.O. Box 361, Stanhope, NJ 07874. Send them a business-size SASE when you write to them.

The Braille alphabet, including both letters and numbers, is available from the AMERICAN FOUNDATION FOR THE BLIND, 15 West 16th Street, New York, NY 10011.

A free Spanish lesson in an easy-to-read, humorous format, is available from In ONE EAR PRESS, 3527 Voltaire Street, San Diego, CA 92106. Request their free *Border Spanish* lesson.

A chart showing the monthly birthstones free from the JEWELERS OF AMERICA, 1271 Avenue of the Americas, New York, NY 10020.

The Fund Raising Handbook offers ideas and instructions for money raising events and programs. Request booklet number

342 from SPERRY & HUTCHINSON COMPANY, Consumer Services Department, P.O. Box 4656, Norcross, GA 30091.

Send a business-size SASE stamped envelope to UNITED VAN LINES, Consumer Services Department, 1 United Drive, Fenton, MO 63026 for a free copy of their booklet *How to Hold a Garage Sale.*

NASA has several free books available on space exploration. Among recent titles are *Space Shuttle Facts*, *What About UFO's?*, *All About the Moon*, *America's Spaceport*, *Space Launch Vehicles*, and *Exploring Inner Planets*. Request them from the Public Affairs Office, JOHN F. KENNEDY SPACE CENTER, NASA, Cape Canaveral, FL 32899.

Information on the Space Station is a free booklet offered by MCDONNELL DOUGLAS Space Station, Educational Services Department, P.O. Box 14526, Saint Louis, MO 63178.

Steps to the Moon discusses man's first space conquest, landing on the moon. Write to the U.S. DEPARTMENT OF THE INTERIOR, Geological Survey, Text Products, 604 South Pickett Street, Alexandria, VA 22304.

The U.S. Marine Corps offers a booklet discussing the history of the U.S. flag and the rules you should follow in handling it. Request *How to Respect and Display Our Flag* from the U.S. MARINE CORPS, Department of the Navy, Washington, D.C. 20380.

For a free copy of the Bill of Rights, write to Bill of Rights, PHILIP MORRIS COMPANIES, INC., 2020 Pennsylvania Avenue Northwest, Suite 533, Washington, D.C. 20006, or call (800) 552-2222, or write to VETERANS OF FOREIGN WARS National Headquarters, Veterans of Foreign Wars Building, Kansas City, MO 64111.

A room-by-room full-color photo tour of the White House is free from The White House, Washington, D.C. 20500. Ask for the *White House Tour Booklet.*

The life of George Washington is discussed in a booklet available from WASHINGTON NATIONAL INSURANCE COM-

PANY, Consumer Education Department, Evanston, IL 60201. Request *George Washington and the American Revolution.*

American Indians Today: Answers to Your Questions discusses various Native American tribes. This free booklet is available from the U.S. Department of the Interior, BUREAU OF INDIAN AFFAIRS, Washington, D.C. 20242.

The FEDERAL RESERVE BANK OF NEW YORK, Publications Office, 33 Liberty Street, New York, NY 10045, has available a catalog of their publications, many of which are free. Two that are currently available are *The Story of Checks* and *The Story of Money.*

The UNITED NATIONS has a packet of materials which examine the role of the United Nations, what it is, and how it works. Write to the DEPARTMENT OF PUBLIC INFORMATION, United Nations, New York, NY 10017.

Educational materials on U.S. railroads are available by writing to the ASSOCIATION OF AMERICAN RAILROADS, 1920 "L" Street Northwest, Washington, D.C. 20036, or to SANTA FE RAILROAD LINES, Public Relations Department, 80 East Jackson Boulevard, Chicago, IL 60604.

Information on energy is available from several sources. For free booklets on wind, nuclear, coal, oil, geothermal, and other types of energy, request the *Energy Information Series* from AMERICAN PETROLEUM INSTITUTE, Publications Section, 2101 "L" Street Northwest, Washington, D.C. 20037.

More energy information is available from EXXON, 1251 Avenue of the Americas, New York, NY 10020. Request their *Energy Outlook Series.*

UNION OIL is offering a free booklet called *Geothermal Energy.* Request it from Corporate Communications, Union Oil of California, P.O. Box 7600, Los Angeles, CA 90051.

Nuclear energy is the subject of an information package offered by the U.S. DEPARTMENT OF ENERGY, P.O. Box 62, Oak Ridge, TN 37830. Ask for their "Nuclear Energy Information Package."

The U.S. COUNCIL FOR ENERGY AWARENESS, P.O. Box 66080, Washington, D.C. 20035, is also offering a free booklet on nuclear energy.

Coal Facts is an information package of books and posters about coal. It's free from the NATIONAL COAL ASSOCIATION, Education Department, Coal Building, 1130 17th Street Northwest, Washington, D.C. 20036.

Write to BETHLEHEM STEEL CORPORATION, Bethlehem, PA 18016, for free copies of *Steel: A Picture Story*, and *Steelmaking and the Environment.*

The Story of Aluminum and Alcoa is available from ALCOA, 1501 Alcoa Building, Pittsburgh, PA 15219.

The FOREST SERVICE, U.S. Department of Agriculture, P.O. Box 2417, Washington, DC 20013, is offering two free books: *Enemies of the Forest*, which discusses forest fires, and *Making Paper from Trees.*

The Story of Cotton is a book and poster set available for free from the NATIONAL COTTON COUNCIL, P.O. Box 12285, Memphis, TN 38112.

How milk is made is discussed in *The Handbook of Milking*, a free booklet available from De Laval Agricultural Division, ALFA-LAVAL, INC., 11100 North Congress Avenue, Kansas City, MO 64153.

For a booklet on how rubber is made, request *Firestone in Liberia* from FIRESTONE TIRE AND RUBBER, Public Relations Department, Akron, OH 44317.

The Story of the Redwood Forest is an informative free booklet available from Service Library, CALIFORNIA REDWOOD ASSOCIATION, 1 Lombard Street, San Francisco, CA 94111.

Three excellent free booklets are available from the Public Affairs Office, HARVARD SMITHSONIAN CENTER FOR ASTROPHYSICS, 60 Garden Street, Cambridge, MA 02138. Ask them for *Life in the Universe*, *Comets*, and *Meteorites.*

The NATIONAL OCEANIC AND ATMOSPHERIC ADMINISTRATION, Central Logistics Supply Center, 619 Hardesty Street,

Kansas City, MO 64124. Offers informative booklets on weather including *The Lightening Book, Tornado Warning*, and *Hurricane Warning*.

TWA, INC., Public Relations, 605 3rd Avenue, New York, NY 10158, has several free booklets on flight. Request *How an Airplane Flies, The Airport, 50 Years of TWA Aircraft,* and *The Big Bird Flight Story*.

The Wright Brothers is a free booklet available from WRIGHT BROTHERS NATIONAL MEMORIAL, Route 1, Box 675, Manteo, NC 27954.

The 15th century genius Leonardo da Vinci and his inventions are the subject of a booklet by IBM, Old Orchard Road, Armonk, NY 10504. IBM also offers another free booklet that explains how computers work, titled *About Computers*.

Perhaps the best way to find out if free books are available is simply to ask. If you are interested in a product, call or write to its manufacturer and ask if they have any material that they can send to you. If you want to know about something's history, contact a company or organization that deals with it now; they will likely know all about its past, too.

Book Clubs

Open any magazine and you will find advertisements for book clubs that cater to all sorts of readers. We have seen ads for mystery book clubs, home repair book clubs, paperback book clubs, and many others. The deals these clubs offer certainly look like money-savers. But are they really good values?

DOUBLEDAY BOOK CLUB, 6550 East 30th Street, P.O. Box 6340, Indianapolis, IN 46209-9413, recently advertised a membership offer. Where a new member receives seven books, chosen from the promotional list, and pays $.99 plus shipping and handling. In exchange, you agree to buy six additional books at the club's regular price, often at 40 percent less than what you'd pay in a bookstore. Their typical book costs approximately $12, compared with the usual publishers' price of $20. If you buy only what the agreement requires, you will end up with thirteen books at around $7 each, including shipping and handling. This amounts to a substantial savings on first-quality, new, hardcover books.

Doubleday's sister book club, THE LITERARY GUILD, 6550 East 30th Street, P.O. Box 6330, Indianapolis, IN 46209-9453, offers a similar plan. You start off buying five books for $2, plus shipping and handling. You are then obligated to buy four more, at regular club prices, to fulfill your membership agreement. With an average club price of $20, you end up receiving nine books at around $10 each. Although Doubleday's plan offers a larger discount, these savings are still substantial.

Some book clubs offer further incentives to keep you from dropping your membership once you've fulfilled your purchase obligation. BOOK-OF-THE-MONTH CLUB, for instance, offers a program called B-O-M-C Dividends. Each book you purchase after completing your membership agreement earns you "dividend" points, which can be redeemed against heavily discounted selected books. A recent issue of their B-O-M-C Dividends catalog listed *The New York Times Cookbook* for $6.25, a 75 percent savings off the publisher's price, and *The Five-Minute Flower Arranger* for $5, 68 percent off the publisher's price. For more information, write to Book-of-the-Month Club, Camp Hill, PA 17011-9901.

Book clubs tailored to specific interests are often advertised in related magazines. Look in business magazines for clubs tailored to business people, in cooking magazines for clubs designed for more domestic interests.

BUSINESSWEEK BOOK CLUB features books on a variety of business-related topics. Write to McGraw-Hill, Inc., Blue Ridge Summit, PA 17214-9988, for more information.

More business and finance books are available through FORTUNE BOOK CLUB, which is operated by Book-of-the-Month Club, Inc., Camp Hill, PA 17011-9903.

Fans of mystery novels may want to consider MYSTERY GUILD, another sister club to Doubleday, but devoted solely to mysteries. You can request information on this club by writing to Mystery Guild, 6550 East 30th Street, P.O. Box 6362, Indianapolis, IN 46206-6362.

THE NATURAL SCIENCE BOOK CLUB, a division of Newbridge Communications, Inc., Delran, NJ 08075, focuses on books of scientific interest. Subjects range from global warming to ancient civilizations.

Do-it-yourselfers might be interested in the POPULAR SCIENCE BOOK CLUB, 1716 Locust Street, Des Moines, IA 50336. Featuring books on crafts and home repair, this club bills itself as "the number one do-it-yourself book club."

THE HOW-TO BOOK CLUB, from McGraw-Hill, caters to similar interests. Write to The How-To Book Club, Blue Ridge Summit, PA 17294-0800 for details.

Another choice for home repair buffs is Rodale's PRACTICAL HOMEOWNERS BOOK CLUB. Write to them at P.O. Box 10852, Des Moines, IA 50336.

Crafts are the subject of books offered by the BETTER HOMES AND GARDENS CRAFTS CLUB, 1716 Locust Street, Des Moines, IA 50380-4724. Recent offerings included *The Calligraphy Work Book, Floral Needlepoint,* and *Scroll Saw Country Patterns.*

A division of Book-of-the-Month Club, HOME STYLE BOOKS features cooking, gardening, and craft books. For more information, write to Home Style Books, Camp Hill, PA, 17011-9969.

There are even book clubs for children. THE BEGINNING READERS' PROGRAM, P.O. Box 1772, Sherman Turnpike, Danbury, CT 06816, offers the popular Dr. Seuss books and others to its members.

Flip through magazines that interest you for special offers from these and other book clubs. If you find one that features titles you want, it may be worth joining. But read the offer carefully; make sure the required future purchases are reasonable, and that the regular prices seem fair. Remember, too, that the special "get six books for $.99" offers are only good deals if the six books are ones you want. Otherwise, you're throwing money down the mailbox.

A recent development in book buying is the in-store book club. These clubs offer their members a percentage discount on purchases made in their stores or from their catalogs.

For instance, WALDENBOOKS offers a Preferred Reader program. After paying an annual fee of $5, members get 10 percent off all books purchased. Additionally, for every $100 you spend, Waldenbooks sends you a coupon good for $5 worth of merchandise, with no required purchase beyond that. If you usually spend over $50 a year in retail bookstores, this can be a worthwhile arrangement. For more information, visit your local Waldenbooks store, call (800) 322-2000, or write to Waldenbooks Preferred Reader Customer Service, Department 55, P.O. Box 10218, Stamford, CT 06904.

Books by Mail

Discounts are also available without a club membership. Look for local bookstores, often chains, that offer regular discounts off the regular prices of their merchandise. CROWN BOOKS offers 10 percent off all paperback books and magazines, and 20 percent off all hardback books. Bestsellers and other selected books are discounted even more heavily, with some books marked down to $1. We always check to see if Crown carries a book we're interested in; their discounts are worth it.

If you can't find a discount bookstore nearby, you can still save money on your book purchases. Discount book catalogs offer comparable savings. You have to pay for shipping and handling, but you will most likely avoid paying your state's sales tax on your purchases.

Perhaps the best known of these is BARNES & NOBLE, the New York bookstore. In addition to their New York locations, Barnes & Noble publishes frequent book sale catalogs. Not all of the books in the catalog are on sale, but many are, and at substantial discounts. Write for a free catalog to Barnes & Noble, 126 5th Avenue, New York, NY 10011, or call (201) 767-7079.

STRAND BOOK STORE is another good source for solid discounts of up to 80 percent on a variety of first-quality books. For their latest catalog, write to them at 828 Broadway, New York, NY 10003, or call them at (212) 473-1452.

PUBLISHERS CENTRAL BUREAU, 1 Champion Avenue, Avenel, NJ 07131, features books (and recordings) at up to 83 percent off the regular price. Write for their catalog or call them at (201) 382-7600.

Libraries

You may not have thought of public libraries as a source of free books, but that is indeed what libraries are. For the few minutes it takes to fill out an application for a library card, you can have access to thousands of books—albeit on a temporary basis—for free. Books and other library materials, including magazines, records, and tapes, can be checked out for two, three, or four weeks at a time. Not counting renewal periods. If your local library doesn't have the books you need, they may even track them down for you at other libraries and have them sent.

Public libraries are a great resource for novels, which are usually read only once before we tire of them and relegate them to a shelf to gather dust. Why spend $20+ on a book when we can read the same book, borrowed from a library, for free? Parents, especially, can save a bundle simply by borrowing books for their children instead of buying them. Why pay for books, especially those that will soon lose their interest and appeal, when you can borrow them for free?

How about a book club that offers its books for free? That's exactly what many library systems offer. Our Los Angeles County Public Library system has Books-By-Mail. You make a selection from a catalog of titles (including adventure, mystery, fiction, humor, novels, romance, cooking, large print, books in Spanish, non-fiction, and children's books), send in a pre-paid order card and they will send you back your selection(s). If your title is in circulation and not available, they will keep your request on file and mail it to you as soon as possible. All you have to do is save the shipping materials and mailing label and return the books within 1 month. It's easy, it's convenient and it's free. This is a great service for folks who are homebound, persons in convalescent homes and rural dwellers who do not have a convenient branch library nearby. Ask if this service is available from your library.

Your local library probably offers another great deal, too. When books and magazines become worn, or when editions are superseded by more recent ones, they are withdrawn from circulation. Some libraries sell these books for nominal fees to raise money, but often the libraries just give them away—for free. Ask your librarian if the library has any "withdrawn" books to be given away, and don't be surprised to find real jewels among them. We have discovered everything from best-selling novels to expensive reference books at our local library. Without spending a dime, you can fill your shelves with old leather-bound volumes, nonfiction, and favorite fiction books.

If your local library's selection is limited, or if you are a truly voracious reader, you may wish to consider joining a private library. Though there is a charge to join, those of us who devour books may find this a good way to cut the bill from the bookstore. Once you pay a membership fee and establish a small postage fund, you are sent monthly listings of the library's new acquisitions. You let them know what books you're interested in and how frequently you'd like them sent. The library then sends you your books on a regular basis, deducting postage and handling charges from your postage fund. When you are done with the books, you mail them back to the library.

The best-known private library is probably the NEW YORK SOCIETY LIBRARY, 53 East 79th Street, New York, NY 10021, (212) 288-6900. Out-of-towners can borrow from their 200,000-volume collection, which reaches back to their establishment in

1754, for an annual membership fee. The fee is currently $80, with an additional $15 deposit for postage and handling charges.
  THE MERCANTILE LIBRARY ASSOCIATION, 17 East 47th Street, New York, NY 10017, (212) 755-6710, has a similar collection of books. They are a general lending library, founded by merchants in 1820. Best-sellers, biographies, and mysteries are their specialty. The Mercantile Library's current membership fee is $45 per year; for the cost of two or three new hardback books, you will have access to over 200,000 volumes, available for loan by mail.
  These private libraries are not for everybody. The membership fees are steep, and postage charges can add up. If you do enough reading to make up for the fees, they can help you save money without sacrificing your reading pleasure.
  With all of the free and almost-free books out there, you should never have to buy a book for full price. You may not have to buy it at all.

SAVINGS ON MOVIES, CASSETTE TAPES, AND CD'S

Our two golden rules about books apply to recordings of music and movies as well. If you use our tips, you should never have to pay full price for records, audio cassettes, compact discs, or videotapes. You may not have to pay anything at all. It is possible to earn substantial savings on home entertainment, if you know how.

Clubs: Do They Really Save You Money?

If you've ever read a magazine, you've seen ads for record, audio cassette, and compact disc clubs. Lately, video tape clubs have been added to the list, too. They work like book clubs. Choosing from the list in their advertisement, you select a number of items for next to nothing, and agree to buy additional items within a specified period of time. Is it worth joining these clubs? Upon examining these offers, we feel that they can be good deals—if you read the offers carefully.

COLUMBIA HOUSE, 1400 North Fruitridge Avenue, Terre Haute, IN 47811, is the most well-known of these clubs. A recent advertisement offered 10 compact discs for $6.96 plus shipping and handling, if you commit to buying five more within three years at their regular club prices. (Their prices range from $12.98 to $15.98 each, somewhat higher than regular retail.) In all, the 15 compact discs will cost you around $102—or about $6.80 each. With the retail prices of compact discs running at about $13 in stores, you end up saving almost 50 percent.

They have a similar plan for records and audio cassettes. For $3.99 plus shipping and handling, and a commitment to buy seven more at their regular price of approximately $10, Columbia House will send 15 cassettes. This works out to a total cost of around $100 for the 22 cassettes—about $4.55 each. Once again, this is a 50 percent savings over regular retail prices.

Once your commitment has been met, you are eligible for Columbia House's bonus plan. Each record or cassette purchased at regular price earns another one for free, each compact disc earns another at 50 percent off.

Another national music club is BMG MUSIC SERVICE, 6550 East 30th Street, Indianapolis, IN 46219-1194. They offer the same agreement regardless of whether you order compact discs or audio cassettes. For half of their regular price for one album, plus shipping and handling, they will send eight. (Regular prices currently range from $8.98 to $9.98 for cassettes, and from $14.98 to $15.98 for compact discs.) They do not require any further purchase. This works out to approximately $15 for eight cassettes—$1.88 each—or $18 for eight compact discs—$2.25 each. The savings here are more substantial: 83 percent off retail for compact discs, 79 percent for cassettes, making them almost free.

The catch here is written in the fine print. The Columbia House offer requires a major commitment to buy additional albums at the club's regular prices, which are higher than what you would pay in stores, plus shipping and handling charges. When the extra required purchase is figured in, your savings start to dwindle and their "bonus plan" doesn't do much to help. Instead, look for clubs like BMG Music Service, that do not obligate you to buy additional albums. You can join, get your eight cassettes or compact discs, and walk away with substantial savings.

Movie fans have probably noticed that video cassette clubs are beginning to pop up, too. As with music clubs, they offer tempting packages to new members. But with the number of video rental stores on the rise, they may not be as tempting as they at first appear.

The COLUMBIA HOUSE VIDEO CLUB, 1400 North Fruitridge Avenue, Terre Haute, IN 47812, recently offered eight movies for $34.82 (including shipping and handling) to new members. But the club then requires the purchase of four additional movies at the club's regular prices, which currently range from $29.95 to $79.95, plus shipping and handling. If the additional movies purchased are all priced at $29.95, the final bill is brought to over $160 for 12 tapes, or approximately $13.50 for each. Not a bad deal if you would otherwise buy the videotapes at a retail store.

Loans and Rentals

If you plan on watching movies only once, you are probably much better off finding a video rental store nearby, and renting the movies. For around $2 per night each, you can choose from thousands of movies available for rental.

Shop around for the best rental rates. We have found major differences between stores in rental rates for the same movie. Some stores may offer a lower rate, but insist that the tape be returned earlier than is convenient. Others may cost a bit more, but allow you to keep the film for more time. A few minutes spent with your local yellow pages and a telephone can make renting your favorite movies much more pleasant, and can save you money. Look for midweek specials on children's, science fiction, horror, action movies or musicals. Some video stores offer a 2 for 1 night once a week. New or current releases will probably cost you more since they are in the greatest demand.

Even better, check with your local public library. Many of them now rent out videotapes for free. Their selection is probably not as extensive as your local video stores', but it should keep you busy for some time. Our local library always has a good selection of children's titles and films appropriate for the whole family. Libraries will also add new videos if they are frequently requested.

Other Money-Savers

In addition to retail/rental stores, discount stores, clubs, and libraries, there are other alternatives to saving money on home entertainment cassettes and videos. Some of these may take a little more time and require going out of our way, but in the long run they will end up saving dollars.

Most of us, when we want to buy a particular tape or compact disc, simply head for the nearest chain outlet, assuming that prices are relatively constant. But that is not the case. Prices for the same albums can vary considerably from one store to another. Comparison-shopping will save you money.

Check your local newspaper's inserts or Sunday entertainment section for sales on recordings. Every week we find cut prices on popular and lesser-known artists, and often one store's price is several dollars lower than it's competitors'. Don't ignore general merchandise stores, either. A recent check of a TARGET STORE circular turned up top-of-the-chart favorite cassettes at $3.49 to $6.99 each. Classical compact discs were featured in the same insert at $3.33 each—much lower than regular retail.

As an alternative to new, relatively expensive recordings, many people purchase used recordings. Garage sales are a popular source for used recordings, and you may find some really great deals, particularly on older or obscure recordings. But they are risky and time-consuming. There is often no way to test your finds for warping or scratches, and no guarantee that you'll come across the recordings you want. Large community swap meets with several dozen booths offer a better opportunity of coming across some forgotten musical treasures. Sometimes you can find collectors of old recordings who have literally hundreds of items to swap or sell.

More expensive but safer, retail outlets selling used records have been around for years, and being joined by used compact disc outlets. Your best bet here, in fact, may be in used compact discs, as they are more durable and damage less easily than records—and thus are easier to buy with confidence.

These stores act as exchange clubs. People bring in their unwanted but saleable recordings and receive cash or a store credit. The records and compact discs are then resold for less than their as-new prices. The stores usually offer facilities for you to take a test-listen of your potential purchases, to check for scratches and defects.

As with everything else, compare prices for the best deals. Some sell all titles for the same price; others base their prices on the albums' popularity and condition. COMPACT DISC-COUNT, in Los Angeles, sells all used compact discs for $10. Bring in a used CD that you no longer want, and they'll pay you $5 for it, no matter what the title is. CD BANZAI!, another Los Angeles store, sells most of their used compact discs for $8.88; some for more, some for less. They pay $3 to $4 cash for used CDs, or offer a $5 to $6 store credit.

Check your local telephone directory under "records, tapes, and compact discs" to find a store near you that sells used recordings. If you don't mind buying them used, and if you can find the albums you want, you can build an impressive collection for a minimal investment.

FREE TO ALL PURCHASERS OF "THE MORE FOR YOUR MONEY GUIDES"

New and exciting free and deeply discounted offers are always being initiated and old ones rediscovered. To keep you informed and up-to-date on all the latest and best free offers and methods that you can take advantage of, we are offering all purchasers of our *More For Your Money Guides* a free issue of our "Best Things in Life for Free" newsletter.

Don't miss out on the newest and most innovative free opportunities available to you. Just send a self-addressed, stamped envelope to:

"Best Things in Life for Free"
P.O. Box 6661
Malibu, CA 90265

Some of the best things in life can be free! We are dedicated to providing the most fantastic, undiscovered and overloaded ideas and methods to obtain free goods, products and services for you and your family, and to alert you to the many opportunities to live, travel and enjoy life with little or no money. And, best of all, this information is free to our readers, just for asking.

Also perhaps you've also already had success with ideas of your own that have worked for you, that I haven't included in this book. If so, I would very much like to hear from you. Not only will sharing your ideas and successes be beneficial to others, but we will also pay $100 to the first person sending in an idea or method that we use in subsequent editions of our books, and $50 if it is used in our newsletter.

Additional *More For Your Money Guides* Available From Probus Publishing

How to Go to College for Free, Linda Bowman,
  Order #219, $9.95

How to Fly for Free, Linda Bowman,
  Order #217, $9.95

Freebies (and More) for Folks Over 50, Linda Bowman,
  Order #218, $9.95

Forthcoming Titles

Free Stuff for Your Pet, Linda Bowman,
  Order #271, $9.95

Free Stuff for Kids and Parents Too!, Linda Bowman,
  Order #272, $9.95

USE ORDER FORM ON NEXT PAGE TO ORDER!

ORDER FORM

Quantity	Order #	Title	Price

Payment: MasterCard/Visa/American Express accepted. When ordering by credit card your account will not be billed until the book is shipped. You may also reserve your order by phone or by mailing this order form. When ordering by check or money order, you will be invoiced upon publication. Upon receipt of your payment, the book will be shipped. Please add $3.50 for postage and handling for the first book and $1.00 for each additional copy.

Subtotal	
IL residents add 7% tax	
Shipping and Handling	
Total	

Credit Card # _____

Expiration Date _____

Name _____

Address _____

City, State, Zip _____

Telephone _____

Signature _____

Mail Orders to:

PROBUS PUBLISHING COMPANY
1925 N. Clybourn Avenue
Chicago, IL 60614

or Call:

1-800 PROBUS-1

N00